The Nuts & Bolts
of Christian Education

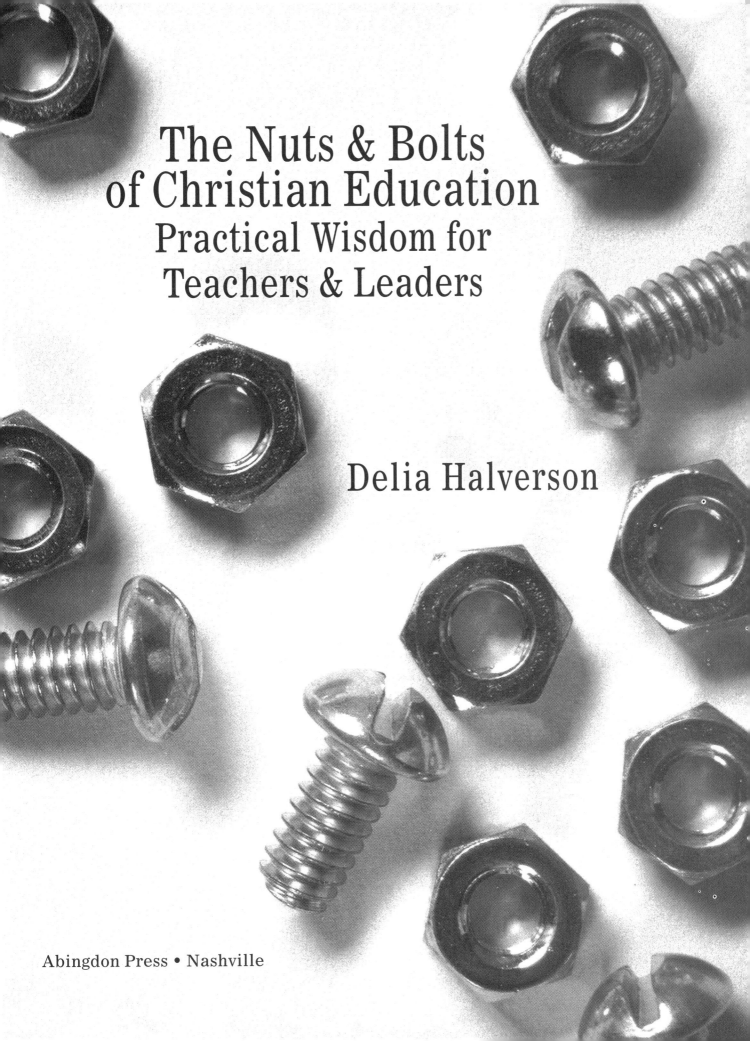

The Nuts & Bolts of Christian Education
Practical Wisdom for Teachers & Leaders

Delia Halverson

Abingdon Press • Nashville

THE NUTS AND BOLTS OF CHRISTIAN EDUCATION
PRACTICAL WISDOM FOR TEACHERS AND LEADERS

Library of Congress Cataloguing-in-Publication Data

Halverson, Delia Touchton.
   The nuts & bolts of Christian education : practical wisdom for teachers and leaders / Delia Halverson.
     p. cm.
   Includes bibliographical references and index.
   ISBN 0-687-07116-X (alk. paper)
   1. Christian education—Handbooks, manuals, etc. I. Title: Nuts and bolts of Christian education. II. Title.

BV1471.2 .H365 2000
268'.6—dc21

00-057629

00 01 02 03 04 05 06 07 08 09—10 9 8 7 6 5 4 3 2 1

MANUFACTURED IN THE UNITED STATES OF AMERICA

Contents

100202

Introduction ———————————————————

Everywhere I go I'm asked, "Can you give me the book that will tell me how to _do_ Christian Education?"

Everyone knows that no book can answer every question because each answer must reflect each specific situation. And I certainly do not have the knowledge to write "the book" that tells exactly how to do Christian education in your congregation.

So why try to write a Christian education manual? Because in my own experience I've found many ideas and helps through networking with other Christian educators, as well as through books and magazine articles on various subjects. But often when I need the information, I can't seem to put my finger on the book it's in, my filing system has broken down, or a particular magazine article is not where I thought it was. Part of my hope with this book is to gather many of these thoughts and themes together in one place. In addition, I hope to get your creative juices flowing so that you can come up with your own answers instead of spending time searching for answers in various books and articles.

In recent years, many Christian education staffs include persons without formal training who are searching for basic guidance. If this describes you, then, I hope, this book will provide practical solutions and point you in the right direction. In addition, I encourage you to take advantage of the numerous training opportunities available in the area of Christian education. Chapter 8 offers several suggestions.

As a first step to using this resource, get acquainted with the table of contents since the arrangement of material does not follow a "here-is-what-you-do-first" format. Of course, reading the entire book will be beneficial to you, but unfortunately few people have the luxury of time to read a book from cover to cover. An index is provided to help you locate the specific topics. In addition, the resource section provides more detailed information about the books referred to throughout the book, as well as other titles that may be helpful in your work.

If you are new on the job, whether you are new to Christian education or simply new to your specific church, I'd suggest reading the section on "Awareness" in chapter 1. This section provides basic information you'll want to know about your new ministry situation.

On the other hand, if you have worked in Christian education for many years, you may find that a few of the ideas listed here are already ingrained into your day-to-day work. However, you will also find new ideas that have been gleaned from my visits to churches across the country. Unfortunately, I did not keep accurate records of where each idea originated, so you may find a suggestion that began with you or in your church. I thank you for that idea. Rest assured that your idea has been shared with others who have found it useful in their ministry, and consider yourself a partner in the writing of this book, which will continue to help churches grow in the purpose that God has set before them. And that is our goal as Christian leaders.

Activities, Alternatives, and Awareness

Awareness

One of the first things that you will want to do when embarking on a new job in Christian education, whether it be your first job or your fifth, is to get to know the people with whom you will be working. Relationships are of primary importance in this job. By failing to establish key relationships early on, you will begin to feel like a frustrated Lone Ranger wandering through the wilderness looking for the campfire. One of the best ways I've found to increase my awareness of people in the church is to use two pictorial directories. One I keep on top of my desk for everyday use. The other I file. In the second book, beside each photo, I record miscellaneous information I glean about the person, such as a recent death in the family, an illness, a career choice, a hobby, an accomplishment or honor, and church responsibilities held in the past. I prefer the book to a computer file because of the photos, and it's more portable. This not only helps me get to know the person but it is a great tool for helping people find their place in the teaching ministry of the church.

You will also benefit from attending as many group events as you can in the first few months in a new position. The more exposure you have the better you will become acquainted with members and potential volunteers. People are hesitant to volunteer to work with someone that they do not know.

Make a point of setting up listening groups. A listening group is a small number of persons with whom you will meet regularly to listen to their thoughts and comments concerning the particular area of the church in which they are involved. The participants in a listening group should change each quarter so that you have an opportunity to listen to as many people as possible in the congregation. Consider listening groups of parents of specific ages, persons who use the library, adult class members, singles, and so forth. The group possibilities are endless. Extend personal invitations to each person, and keep the gatherings informal. Strive to reach a cross section of the congregation.

Some jobs within Christian education are all-encompassing, involving all aspects of CE in the church, while others are more defined, such as working with a certain age level or specific area of ministry. However, unless your responsibility is limited to teaching one age level in a classroom, you will be working with adults and must understand their needs. Even if your responsibility is to children or youth ministry, adult workers will still form the backbone of your ministry. You must be aware of the lifestyles of the members of your church. Are there working parents, one parent families, stay-at-home moms or dads, college students, never-married singles, divorced, widowed, semi-retired, or retired folks? What type of learning experience is being offered for each of these groups?

Multiple Intelligences

For years Christian educators have professed that we do not all learn in the same manner. Much of our education rests on an ability to evaluate situations in our world and to solve problems associated with those situations. Howard Gardner, an authority on brain research, identified seven intelligences that God gave each of us. No one learns using just one of these intelligences, but often an individual relies more heavily on one intelligence than the others. If we can understand these seven ways of learning, we can better grasp ways to pass our faith on to others. Barbara Bruce's book, *Seven Ways of Teaching the Bible to Children*, offers a variety of ways to apply this theory.

Jesus used these methods of teaching. Listed below are examples from Jesus' ministry.

• *Verbal/Linguistic* refers to language and words, both written and spoken. *Jesus approached listeners in this manner with his stories.*

• *Logical/Mathematical* includes inductive thinking and reasoning, statistics, and abstract patterns. *Jesus used questions and answers to reach his listeners who learned in this way.*

• *Visual/Spatial* deals with visualizing objects and creating mental pictures. *Jesus used common objects to explain his meaning to persons who learn in this manner.*

• *Body/Kinesthetic* relates to the physical, such as movement and physical activity. *Jesus involved the disciples in learning through fishing and washing their feet.*

• *Musical/Rhythmic* involves recognition of patterns, both tonal and rhythmic. *Singing hymns was a part of the common experience of Jesus and his disciples.*

• *Interpersonal* follows relationships between persons, including true communication. *Jesus worked with persons on a personal level and also developed small groups, his most successful group being the twelve disciples.*

• *Intrapersonal* denotes self-reflection and awareness of that within us which guides us. *On many occasions the Bible mentions Jesus drawing away from others for solitude (by himself or with his disciples) or for reflection.*

Age Awareness

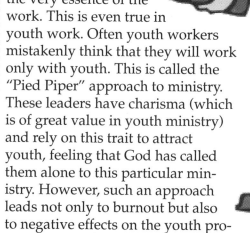

Most jobs in a Christian education program involve a heavy dose of working with adults, both volunteers and parents of children and youth. Therefore, adult volunteers must be relied upon and trained to carry out the very essence of the work. This is even true in youth work. Often youth workers mistakenly think that they will work only with youth. This is called the "Pied Piper" approach to ministry. These leaders have charisma (which is of great value in youth ministry) and rely on this trait to attract youth, feeling that God has called them alone to this particular ministry. However, such an approach leads not only to burnout but also to negative effects on the youth program. When the youth worker moves to another church or discovers that she or he can no longer continue in the job, the program falls apart from lack of a strong framework to support it.

Whatever your position in Christian education, you must recognize the importance of volunteers and allow them to help you build a foundation for the ministry. Understanding adults and how they function is important in every aspect of a teaching and educational ministry. Appendix 1 offers a basic summary of various adult generations. Every adult will not fit neatly into the category assigned to his or her generation. Each of us is a unique person and must be treated as an individual. It is important to recognize generational differences in people, but emphasis should be placed on becoming personally acquainted with your volunteers.

Becoming familiar with the characteristics of various aged children and youth is key if your area of responsibility includes those age groups. However, even if your responsibility lies primarily with adults, many of those adults are parents; and your understanding of their children will be critical to your understanding of them. Appendix 2 provides information on the youth and children's generations. Take time to get acquainted with the children and youth in your church. Stop them in the corridors, talk with them, attend some of their events, visit with them in the lunchroom at school, and listen to the music that they enjoy.

When I conduct a workshop with teachers of children, I use the following activity to help participants see the world through a child's eyes. I ask the teachers to pair off, and I ask one person to squat or sit in front of the person who is standing. The "squatter" is instructed to tell the "stander" what he or she sees from that vantage point. After a short time, the roles are reversed. Afterward teachers understand why suggestions such as mounting pictures at children's eye level and sitting among the children instead of hovering over them are important. I also remind them that when a young child draws a picture of a face, there are usually two eyes and a mouth. And then the child will carefully place two dots in the middle of the face. In reality, children, as they tip their heads back to see us, look right up our noses. If that doesn't help teachers realize that they must get down on the level of the children, not much will! It's difficult to understand children or youth without spending time "walking in their shoes."

Intergenerational Needs

Not so long ago, families lived in the same community with their relatives. There was a great network of family, comprised of all ages. Adult relatives acted as role models and mentors for all of the children. "The village" really did raise the child, even when all the members of the village weren't actually related. Children learned to go to certain adults with certain questions, and it was not always their parents.

Children sometimes now grow up having few if any relationships with adults other than their parents or perhaps the parents of their peers. They often don't see their grandparents more than once a year, and usually for only brief visits. There are virtually no opportunities, outside of the church, that offer intergenerational experiences. This is a need that must be met by the church, not only because children need models and mentors of every generation but also because these multi-age experiences are the best tools for teaching the faith. It has been said that Christianity is one generation from extinction. This is certainly true if we, as church leaders, do not offer these cross-age learning opportunities.

Often a church boasts of being a family church; but once the family steps through the door, children are herded in one direction (dividing them further "according to age and ability"), teenagers in another direction, and adults in still another (again often dividing them according to age). Evaluate how often your church offers intergenerational experiences. Make a list of all of the opportunities offered in the past year to people of all ages to become acquainted in your church. Plan to establish additional intergenerational experiences, considering the following:

• Are children encouraged to attend and participate in the corporate worship, or is their study or gathering time at the same hour as worship?

• Do the tables at church dinners encourage different ages to sit together? Do you have community singing or suggestions for table conversation during the meals? Are birthdays and anniversaries celebrated?

• Do families have opportunity for service with people of all ages, such as working on a mission project, setting the tables for church dinners, visiting

nursing homes, planting and tending a garden for a food pantry, or doing yard or maintenance work around the church?

• Do parents have learning experiences that they share with their children?

Family Classes

Most parents have full-time jobs. Because of this, they highly value their family time; and many do not want to spend two hours away from their children on Sunday morning. Consider organizing a class for parents and children to study together, where the parents and children help one another with designated lessons or topics. As the parents help the children, they remember much of what they have forgotten or that they never had an opportunity to learn as children. Likewise, children can offer their parents different perspectives that help them explore the Bible and faith in new ways.

One church found that a young couple brought their two-year-old to their adult Sunday school class because they hated being away from their child since they both worked all week. In response, the church established a class for parents *and* young children, where parents spent part of the class working with the children and the other part overseeing their children at play but discussing a class topic of their own.

Another church provides a family class for elementary children and their parents during the summer. They adapted the Scouting curriculum, *God and Me*, including the projects that the parents and children do at home. *FaithHome* is another helpful resource for family study. This six-session study ideally includes a meal and extends to two hours for each session, but is easily adapted to shorter periods and additional sessions.

Anti-bias Awareness and Needs

Given the diversity of our communities and neighborhoods, Christian education programs have a greater responsibility to teach cultural and ability awareness than ever before. Our world has grown smaller, and those people who are different from our students aren't "over there" but across the street, and hopefully inside our doors. We need to understand our differences and grow in our appreciation of others, rather than expecting everyone to conform to our actions and our way of thinking. Here are suggestions and questions to think about in order to ensure that your church, childcare program, and preschool are aware of and are learning about other cultures and persons different from themselves:

• What is the ethnic mix of your church? Is everyone included in the various leadership roles throughout the church?

• How can persons of both sexes, other cultures, and with different abilities be used to help the congregation grow in understanding and awareness?

• What activities and items can help children appreciate persons different from and like themselves? Consider different foods, clothing, home-life centers, music, games, bulletin boards and decorations, toys, science projects, dramatic play time, and art. Often school supply catalogs feature items from a number of cultures. Look for crayons and markers in different colors to use for various skin tones, play items (such as puzzles and doll house figures) with persons in wheelchairs, and products in Braille as well as print. Use multicultural foods as snacks. How can aspects of other countries (such as clothing, houses, food) be incorporated into everyday experiences?

• Look for stereotypic materials that can be discarded, changed, or adapted. Are all of the persons doing housework or secretarial work women? Are all of the construction workers men?

• Become alert to language to watch for, avoid, or change. Do you or others use black and white to indicate bad and good? Do you or others refer to *mankind* instead of *humankind*? Are only male pronouns used for God?

• Do pictures depict family life in different social situations and cultures, a balance of men and women doing jobs inside and outside the home?

• Do library books reflect cultural diversity? Do they include persons with disabilities doing everyday activities?

• Do the bulletin boards and pictures in the church indicate that you are an inclusive church, growing in awareness?

• What service projects, field trips, visitors, alternative celebrations and rituals can be incorporated into your teaching ministry?

Think about the various ways your church includes persons with physical and mental challenges.

• Are there ramps leading to the entrance of each building? Do multifloor buildings have elevators?

• Are the doors wide enough to accommodate wheelchairs?

- Are some pews shorter than others in order to accommodate wheelchairs out of the aisles?
- Does the height of tables accommodate wheelchairs?
- Is there adequate room for a wheelchair in the restroom stalls?
- Do you have equipment or designated seating for hearing-challenged persons? Is signing available during worship?
- Is additional classroom help provided for children who are mentally challenged, and a class available for adults who are mentally challenged?
- Are direction signs large enough that those with sight difficulties can see them? Are large print Sunday school books, bulletins, and hymnals available?

Alternatives and Activities (Beyond the Basic Sunday School)

When the concept of Sunday school was first initiated, it was actually a school, established in the factory centers of England where children were made to work six-day weeks instead of going to school. Sunday school began as a ministry to these children, educating them on the only day that they had free. At present, we must use that same concept, the idea of ministering to all those needing it at times that are most convenient for them. This may not always be Sunday morning, and may involve providing educational opportunities at varying times during the week.

You can discover the best times and designs for learning opportunities for children and youth through conversations with their parents. Outlined below are ideas that other churches have used. Remember, however, that you cannot successfully transport someone else's program into your church without adjusting it to meet your particular situation.

Day-Care Programs

Survey your neighborhood to determine whether day-care needs are being met. There are many government regulations necessary for this ministry, and you will need to check your own government agencies. *Weekday Programs for Children*, and *Director's Manual*, by Gloria Thomas offer detailed information on setting up day-

care programs in churches. The manual includes information on everything from budgets to reproducible forms.

Preschool Programs

A morning program for preschoolers has traditionally been one of the first extra programs added by a church in its program for children. With so many dual-career families and children already in day care, take a close look at the feasibility of such a program in your church. The book *Weekday Programs for Children* mentioned above will also help you design this program.

If a preschool program is provided, make no apologies for including Christian concepts and stories in the curriculum. One resource that may be helpful is *Wonder-filled Weekdays*. This resource of lessons with faith connections is in four volumes.

After-School Programs

After-school programs offer a great opportunity to reach new people and involve them in your church. These programs may meet daily or once a week, and often vary in their content. Some churches include religious curriculum, while others simply provide help with homework and play activities. These programs can also give opportunity for retired adults to work with children in a tutoring program, particularly in reading. Churches sometimes contract with a nearby school, and the school provides the curriculum that is used in the program. An after-school program is particularly effective if a school is located nearby or if picking up or dropping off children at your building can be arranged.

Covenant Groups

A covenant group is a small group of people who commit to meeting regularly to "watch over one another in love." The members of a group help each other discern God's direction for their lives and encourage one another in carrying out the goals they set. This covenant movement is a part of the Wesleyan tradition and has been used with youth and children as well as adults. These groups use Wesley's General Rules as categorized through Works of Mercy (acts of compassion and justice) and Works of Piety (acts of devotion and worship).

The following resources for covenant groups are available through Discipleship Resources:

Covenant Discipleship (for adults) by David Lowes Watson

Together in Love (for youth) by David C. Sutherland

Sprouts (for children) by Edie Harris and Shirley Ramsey

Mother's Morning In

While the majority of mothers work outside the home, many have chosen to be stay-at-home moms. Appendix 17 provides a sample format for this type of program. If this particular format is not appropriate for your church, offer some type of affirming ministry and support group for stay-at-home moms or dads. Such programs help with the isolation many often feel because they do not currently choose a career outside the home. These programs also help them to recognize child rearing as a legitimate career choice.

Midweek Dinner and Evening Programs

Many churches find that a midweek dinner offers opportunity for fellowship that is sometimes missed on Sunday mornings, particularly when there are multiple worship services. Here are some suggestions to consider in planning these events.

• When establishing a time, consider working adults, families with young children, and older adults who do not like to drive after dark. This may involve a wide range for the serving time.

• Use round tables or rectangular tables clustered together that invite conversation among diners.

• Provide high chairs and booster seats for children.

• Be mindful of the dietary needs of all persons. In your announcements, state that you will work with special dietary needs if arrangements are made ahead of time. Consider providing an alternative for children who don't like the food on the menu, such as peanut butter and jelly sandwiches. Include milk for the children and those adults who prefer it.

• Although persons will arrive at varying times, set a specific time during the meal for a common blessing and recognition of birthdays, anniversaries, and other announcements. Also, include community singing. Many churches provide conversation starters on a sheet of paper at the center of each table.

• Plan activities for every age group, including infant care and adult classes.

• Provide transportation for persons who do not feel comfortable driving after dark.

• Occasionally plan an event that all ages can enjoy together. This may be a puppet play or a multigenerational craft evening.

Children's Church

Children's church has become a catchall term. Many people prefer not to use the term for a specific program because it implies that children are not welcome in corporate worship. *All* children should be welcome in worship services, but options should be available for preschool and possibly first grade children. These options may include anything from quality child care to additional sessions of study which are different from the lesson during a Sunday school hour. Older preschoolers and first graders may attend part of the service and then move into a classroom for the remainder of the time. *Children's Church Times* is a good resource to use with preschoolers and first graders. It is published in four volumes with twenty-six weekly lessons of thirty to sixty minutes.

It is very important that elementary children be a part of the worship service. Their experienced and affiliated styles of faith are active, and they need to feel that they are a part of the community of faith. Worship is one of our opportunities for experiencing God, and there is much in the worship service that children can experience with understanding. There is a window of opportunity during the first couple of elementary years when a child is anxious to be a part of the parent's activities, and it is important not to miss that time. This is the time to "set" the habit of attending worship.

Sometimes churches provide a minichurch service for children, where the regular worship service is duplicated with ushers, offering, and so forth. Instead of duplicating a service that already exists, involve the children in actually assisting the ushers in the corporate worship and also involve them in an elementary worship study. A good resource for this type of study is *Children Worship* by MaryJane Pierce Norton. After such a study, be sure to plan a recognition for the students in the worship service as they become a more active part of the worshiping community.

Another aid to helping children worship is a *young reader's bulletin*. This differs from most children's bulletins in that it is created each week and follows the pattern of the adult bulletin. It contains explanations of the different parts of worship and provides spaces for children to fill in information they learn by being aware of what is happening around them. Appendix 3 offers a sample of a Young Reader's Bulletin.

Summer Events

Summer is a great time to plan special events. Since families often take extended trips during the summer, advertise your plans well in advance to allow them opportunity to plan around them. Consider scheduling several events throughout the summer so that every family can take advantage of at least one or more of the activities. Listed below are several ideas that churches have used successfully. Here again, remember to design events according to your own church and community needs and schedules.

• Vacation Bible school can be held during the morning or at night. Many churches find it more convenient to have sessions at night and to include a meal and classes for youth and adults. Some churches have even designed a weekend VBS. The original concept of VBS was to offer a learning experience during the summer, when children were bored with so much free time. Now children have numerous day-camp opportunities, and families often spend longer periods away from home than in the past. Consequently, creativity in planning your program is critical.

In one church where I worked, we once found ourselves in the midst of a building program during the summer and unable to use the facility for VBS. Instead of the traditional program, we wrote a curriculum for a "Backyard Bible School" that the parents then used with their children. We held a mini training event for the parents on a Sunday before the beginning of the summer, where we distributed the materials and gave parents an opportunity to learn the songs and experiment with the crafts. Several families got together and enjoyed the learning experiences as a group. Others chose to work as individual families. Some spread the learning experience over the summer, and a few even took the curriculum along on their vacation trips. At the end of the summer we held a big celebration during worship, sharing the entire experience with the congregation.

VBS has always been a tool for inviting unchurched children in the community to participate in church. Find ways to publicize your event, and make it a welcoming experience for those who are not regular members of your church.

• *Marketplace* is a program that many churches have used for an expanded study opportunity during the summer. This program usually involves several mornings or evenings, or a weekend. Some churches have used it for a full day of family learning on Saturday. Centers are set up to offer learning experiences that introduce the participants to life in Bible times. Each person is assigned to a "tribe" that includes children and adults. The tribes take turns visiting the centers which might include:

the well	where they get their water for the day in gallon jugs
synagogue school	where they learn to write a few words in Hebrew
potter's shed	where they experiment in making pottery
market	where they try various foods typical of the era
storyteller	where they hear stories of our biblical heritage

Curriculum for Marketplace is available, and can be purchased through most Christian bookstores.

• *A mission study* gets very little time during the usual Sunday school curriculum, and summer is a good opportunity to expand this area of learning. This can be done through several short experiences or an extended time. Hands-on mission experiences are important, and there are ample opportunities available for older children, youth, and adults.

One church planned a mission field trip each week during the summer, visiting soup kitchens, nursing homes, recycling centers, and such. Prior to each visit they studied about the type of mission they were visiting and worked on a related project. They concluded their visit with a Bible study that also related to the visit. (See "Retreats, Mission Events and Trips" on page 18)

Another church set up a week-long event where elementary children and adult leaders studied about people in countries where the church supported missionaries. They set up centers with food, clothing, games, language, and stories, similar to the Marketplace format above. The children and adults were placed in groups called "Circles of Friends," which visited the various centers throughout the week. They even set up a call on a speaker phone and talked to a missionary. In the food center they made breads in the tradition of the different countries, and these were used for communion at the close of the week.[1]

• *Heritage personalities* can make up a summer study. Your denomination or congregation has significant people in its past that can serve as great role models for children and youth. Contact your denominational offices or a Christian bookstore for curriculum or information for such a study. The eleventh chapter of Hebrews offers a good biblical reference for this study.

• *Musical experiences* are enjoyable during the summer. Children's musicals are available with printed curriculum that can enhance these learning events. If held during the summer, it may be helpful to condense the experience into one week. Such an event requires consistent attendance, and many families are unable to attend on a week-to-week basis during the summer months.

Whatever you plan during the summer, announce your plans ahead of time and set up a comprehensive registration for all summer events at one time during the spring. Additional names may be added as each event draws near, but if the basic registration is held early and one registration form is used, then you help parents plan and eliminate the hassle of filling out multiple forms, as well as avoid lots of headaches for yourself. See appendix 11 for an example of this form.

Seasonal and Special Events

Excitement always mounts during our special seasons, and special experiences around the church year make great learning tools. Consider some of the following ideas.

• Teach the symbols of the season at a special event or during a worship service. If a special event is planned, include hands-on opportunities to make various symbols. The learning can take place during a worship service, explaining the various symbols as they are brought into place. One such example is "Hanging of the Greens," which is located in appendix 7.

• Celebrations of baptisms, confirmation, weddings, and other special occasions can be turned into learning events. Look at your church's liturgy for such events, and add a few words of explanation about what is happening. This can be as simple as asking the pastor to explain briefly why we use water for baptism or asking confirmation students to explain banners they created about their understanding of various faith concepts. In one church the confirmation class created an electronic project about their church. They placed photos on a computer disk and added individual statements they had written about what the church meant to them.

• A great time to have a one- or two-day study for children is during the week between Christmas and New Year. This is typically a "down" time for kids, and a short-term study often goes over well at this time.

Intergenerational Involvement

Generally, parents lack opportunities to be with their children; and children and youth have few occasions to interact with senior adults. Multi-age experiences should be a part of every church, but it seldom happens unless the education department promotes such occasions. Some churches have even planned older adult day care and children's day care events so the two groups can interact.

Although there is little curriculum written for such events, elementary material can easily be adapted by involving the parents as assistants during the learning experiences or asking older adults to sit with the children, giving support and loving hugs.

I have often led parent-child retreats where parents and children have met separately during part of the event, and then we have come together for a portion of the learning experience. During the multi-age module, activity centers were set up, including written instructions for what was to be done in a specific center. Families then visited various centers as they wished, following the instructions provided and learning together.

Some churches have established adoptive grandparent programs, which help children who live hundreds of miles from their own grandparents to have personal experiences with persons of other generations. You can develop such a program in a variety of ways, anything from planned activities and meals that children and senior adults share to involving whole families.

Don't overlook spontaneous opportunities for multi-age involvement. These happen during meals, fellowship times before and after worship, special worship times such as Christmas Eve, and church family retreats.

Community Outreach

Churches that recognize the potential for outreach to the community are growing churches. One church used a money gift from an older couple to begin a once-a-week coffee house for the youth in the community. First United Methodist Church in Clermont, Florida, recognized the importance of reaching out to kids in their community and built small skating ramps on their property, carefully following the requirements stated under their insurance policy. Within four months eighty kids registered to skate there, and lives were and are being changed.

The first time I heard about one church's elaborate recreational program I wasn't sure about its relevance. Then I overheard a parent telling how she was in conversation about soccer teams while waiting in a dentist office. The other person was impressed with the healthy attitude of her son's coach and asked where he played. This encounter brought the family to the church, and they became active members.

Review your facility and your community. Perhaps you have property that you can make available to families in your community for small gardens, or maybe a gardening program can be sponsored on a nearby vacant lot. Perhaps community homeowners need a place to hold monthly or annual meetings, and your church has the space. Be sure information about your church is on hand when they meet, and ask a volunteer to be available to answer any questions persons may have about your church and its programs.

A workshop I conducted happened to fall on the same day as the church's big rummage sale. At the sale greeters moved among the crowd and invited persons to tour the facility. During the tour, information about the church was shared, including their various educational and worship opportunities.

Computer Labs/Curriculum

Computer technology in Christian education is exploding. Currently, there are lots of glitzy games and Bible story programs on the market, but many of them entertain more than educate, and few programs are formational (helping children further develop their faith) rather than informational (simply giving information and then quizzing kids on the facts they learned). Consequently, it is important to learn or train teachers to use the programs in creative ways. Working on computers can become such one-student-focused experiences that we sometimes lose the opportunity for group building, which is also important.

Consider beginning your computer experiences by creating a book or newsletter about the subject being studied and then deciding as a group just what will go into such a publication. Divide the children into smaller groups to work on various parts of the book, using a computer to research the information and to write and publish the work. One church did this and expanded the idea by selling the publication to support a mission venture that they planned. Learning and mission go hand-in-hand.

Two resources that I recommend are:
From BC to PC: A Guide for Using Computers with Children in Christian Education by Nancy Spence and Jane Connell
Computers, Kids and Christian Education by Neil MacQueen.

Retreats, Mission Events, and Trips

Although retreats and mission trips are popular among churches, the planning and execution of such events can be overwhelming. The key, then, is organization and advanced planning. Use the forms in appendixes 4 and 5 for planning these events.

Families will grow together in their faith if they serve together in mission. Plan one church-wide mission project per year or offer several and allow families to choose. Projects may include: recycling cans or paper with the proceeds going to missions; collecting used clothing and food pantry items; making food baskets and arranging for families to deliver them; painting or fixing up homes of elderly members; visiting a shut-in on a regular basis; growing a garden for a soup kitchen.

Field trips are popular events for all ages, even adults. Appendix 6 can provide guidance as you plan field trips. Here are a variety of ideas for trips listed by subjects:

God's World
- Walk through a park or woods
- Visit a plant nursery, greenhouse, garden, wheat fields, and so forth
- Plant or tend a garden for an older person

Stewardship of the Earth
- Visit a recycle plant (some will allow free entrance in exchange for spending time collecting trash at a park)
- Take a camera trip around the community to record good or bad stewardship
- Visit a dumping ground, composting site, polluted pond, and so forth

Helpers for God
- Fire or police station
- Hospital or nursing home
- Farm
- Schools

The Hungry
- Soup kitchen
- Gleaning after harvesters (example: The Society of St. Andrew 800-333-4597)
- Food distribution center

The Sick
- Emergency room
- Nursing home
- Clinic
- Blood bank

In Prison
- Local jail or prison
- Courtroom (how does it feel to be accused, sometimes unjustly)

Worship
- Other churches or synagogue
- Your sanctuary (look at symbols)
- Outdoor worship areas

Bible Background for Stories
- Boat trip (Paul's journeys)
- Jail (prison experiences of Peter, Paul, and Silas)
- High tower (Jesus' temptation)
- Sheep farm (shepherd)
- Barren land or desert (Moses and Israelites wanderings)
- Dark place (Jesus as Light)
- Underground area (catacombs)
- Potter's shop (God molds us)
- Beach or lake (Jesus' time by the lake with disciples)
- Building sites (foundations of our faith)

Support Groups

Many support groups already exist in our communities. Certainly, there is no need to duplicate those that are readily available to your church, but it is important to inventory the community to find out what is there. Support groups typically like to remain fairly small, so you may find that another group could be started even though one already exists. Or you may want to offer meeting space within your building for an existing group. Here are some you may want to consider:

Persons suffering from addictions
Weight loss
Expectant and new parents
Parents of teens
Parents of emotionally disturbed children
Parents of children with specific disabilities
Divorce recovery
Single parents
Children of divorced parents (See organization "Rainbows" in Resources and References.)
Blended families
Homosexuals
Persons with recent job loss
Widowed persons
Bereaved children/adults
Stay-at-home moms/dads
Never-married singles
Cancer patients
Caregivers in families
Persons with specific illnesses, such as AIDS, diabetes, and so forth

---

1. Roswell United Methodist Church, Roswell, Georgia.

Chapter 2

Budgets, Buses, and Beads

Sometimes it is the everyday process of ministry that gets us down. We sail along fine when we have special projects in the works, but then suddenly we recognize that in our excitement and concentration on the "big pieces" we have let the little everyday things pile up. Then it's a real chore to try to dig out from under everything. I was once moving from one office to another after the church had completed a building project and loaded several miscellaneous stacks of papers that needed filing into a box, thinking I'd file them after getting settled in my new office. Two years later I discovered the box, untouched. In those two years I had not missed one thing in the box. Even though I could not bring myself to throw the entire box away, most of the items were of no great importance.

Through the years, I've used several methods for organizing my office. Although you will have to develop your own method, I have learned to keep several different sets of files including these:

• **Subject/resource file** with articles and information on various subjects

• **Methods file** with ideas and information on various teaching methods, such as storytelling, music, poetry, puppets, and such

• **Desk work** containing budgets and expense records, committee lists and minutes, job descriptions, teacher lists, curriculum orders, and general information

• **Events** including workshops, conferences, training events, retreats, VBS, and so forth, I organize these files by dates of the events.

This method of dividing the materials into different filing systems has been tremendously helpful. I keep the desk work and events files at my fingertips, and the others can be filed across the room, since I don't need them as frequently and seldom use them when I'm on the phone.

You will certainly need some sort of system for keeping up with what's going on as you plan and carry out ministry experiences and events. The "Planning Checklist" in appendix 8 will help you here. Adjust it to meet your unique needs.

Evaluating and Assessment of Progress

Most people think that evaluation should be the last thing to consider. However, periodically every Christian education program needs to be thoroughly reviewed and evaluated. Immediately after you begin your job and before you set new goals, work with your education committee to evaluate the ministry's effectiveness. Numbers are not as important as what's happening to the people, so avoid an emphasis on attendance unless there has been a drastic decline or increase. Then look for any differences from the past. Appendix 10 provides an example of a review for a children's council, as well as a group evaluation called "Sandwich Evaluation," which is used when I need to pass on a recommendation for change to a teacher. I sandwich the recommendation between two commendations.

Even as new programs and plans are launched, we need to be aware of how we will assess them when they are completed. This can be done through personal interviews, a form asking participants "How did we do?" or by looking at your goals with the program or event committee and determining if they were met and how they might be improved the next time. Keep a written record of all your evaluations, even if you do not plan to repeat the event. This will be useful in the future when planning for other events. In addition, these reviews are helpful for new committee members as they acclimate themselves to the ministry.

Budgets

It is important to involve all members of the education committee in every aspect of the budget request. The entire committee needs to recognize this as their ministry too.

Ensuring that the expenses for Christian education are included in the overall church budget is important for several reasons:

1. It places education as an important aspect of the church.
2. It backs the ministry of the teachers, by saying "We, as a congregation, stand behind you and thank you for your ministry."
3. It enables you to plan with a clear understanding of your resources.
4. It unifies the mission of the church instead of committees vying for funds.

The general rule of thumb is that education (excluding any staff salaries) should be allotted about 2 to 5 percent of the congregation's budget. Sometimes churches hire a Christian educator and then do not provide adequate funds for the work to be carried out. This is poor stewardship of the church budget and resources.

My first time experience with an education budget was baffling. In the first place, I'd had no training in bookkeeping and, other than our very simple household accounts, I'd

never had to deal with keeping a budget. I had been told to just turn in my expenses and the treasurer would write a check to reimburse me for them. I came on the job in June, and so by the time we got ready to "plan the budget" for the next year, I'd had a good bit of expenses run through that year's accounts. When I viewed the year-to-date accounts, I had no idea what expenses had been credited to what accounts because the treasurer's understanding of the budget was different from mine. Supplies for VBS were put under supplies in general, and there was this strange line item that I didn't even know was in my budget! I later found out the line item was for the Boy Scout troop, which I had absolutely no responsibility for at all. I was told, "It had to go somewhere, so we put it in your budget." After a couple of years I insisted that the Boy Scouts have their own account because it made it appear that we had more money in our CE budget than we actually had.

This experience taught me to specify where each expense was to be accounted when I turned the expenses and bills in. If I was to know exactly how much it cost to operate a week of VBS, then I needed to have the supplies for VBS listed under that line-item. And this was important, because it helped us know if we needed to increase registration fees the next year and if we were practicing good stewardship in our VBS.

There were other things that I learned as I grew in my CE experience. I learned what items needed to be included, and I learned how to ask for specific items to be added to my budget. You will find a sample budget in appendix 9. This will not specifically fit your church, but perhaps it will give you some ideas.

Everything we do in the church should be preceded by a sincere discernment of God's purpose. You have already gone through a discernment process similar to that on page 42 as you have made the decision to pursue the project or program. Now you are ready to present it for inclusion in the budget. Continue seeking God's guidance as you develop a presentation to explain the budget needs. Here is my suggestion for steps to use in creating such a presentation.

1. Surround the whole process in prayer, seeking God's guidance as you write the proposal.
2. Read the church mission statement and determine how this program fulfills that mission.
3. List the needs that led to the development of a plan for this program.
4. List persons who will likely participate in the program.
5. List benefits from the program.
6. Lift these needs, persons, and benefits again to God in prayer.
7. With the information from steps 2 to 5 in mind, go back through the church mission statement and underline the parts of the statement that this program fulfills. This underlined mission statement then becomes the foundation for your written presentation.
8. Pull out each of these phrases and print them below the mission statement. Below each phrase, point out ways that the program fulfills that phrase.
9. Write a closing summary, including phrases from the mission statement.

This sort of written statement can accompany a request to a church board or finance committee, or it can be used to help others understand just why such a program is proposed. The following example was developed when a church planned to build a new complex that would house a chapel, gathering room, meeting room, and library. There was debate within the church because this was not the next step in the original long-range plan.

Example:

Hometown Church Mission Statement
Hometown Church is a fellowship of people choosing to follow Jesus Christ by loving others with our hearts, *enriching our souls through worship*, *educating our minds by study*, and *serving God and humanity* with our strengths. We are a *caring community* joined together by a desire *to be a blessing to those around us* and with a wish to be known by the *difference we make in the world*.

Enriching our souls through worship
- The chapel will provide opportunity for small-group worship, including youth worship experiences, weddings, memorial services, worship settings for committees and other groups.
- The chapel may be used for communion each Sunday.
- With a new library in this complex, the old library area can be opened up for added seating in the sanctuary.
- The prayer room will be open for individual opportunities for prayer, thereby emphasizing the importance of prayer undergirding our ministry.
- The courtyard will be appropriate for outdoor worship services with the possibility of opening the doors from the gathering room to enhance and enlarge such worship services.
- The gathering room can be used for informal worship settings.

Educating our minds by study
- The complex will provide several areas that can be used for study: the gathering room, the meeting room, and if necessary the chapel and library.
- The library, being adjacent to the gathering and meeting rooms, will provide resources to be used in preparation for teaching and will encourage reading for all ages.

Loving others, serving God and humanity, making a difference in the world
- The meeting room and gathering room can be available for women's and men's group meetings and other groups and committees as we plan to serve God through the channels where God leads us.
- The added meeting space can open up other areas of our campus so that we may reach out to groups, such as AA, Alanon, and so forth.

Being a caring community, blessing those around us
- The new structure (along with the restructure of the Youth Center) will make a more welcoming approach from the street, with doors opening to the street side of the building. This projects an image of community and gives the message that everyone is welcome at Hometown Church.
- The gathering room can be used for fellowship times after services, thereby giving our members better opportunity to greet and get to know our visitors and guests.

Work on the budget does not end with its preparation and presentation. It is important to monitor it throughout the year. Be mindful that the bills are paid promptly, and that plans for purchasing equipment and other major supplies are developed early and carried out by midyear. Make an earnest effort not to overspend your budget. If you exercise responsibility in handling the budget, then the next year's planning and request process will go much smoother. Of course there will occasionally be a time when additional money will need to be requested. When this situation occurs, involve the entire education committee in documenting the need just as carefully as when the first budget was presented.

Registration Fees

Churches often differ about charging registration fees for programs. Some charge the participants in a program exactly what it costs to run the program, while others charge no registration fee at all and build all expenses into the church budget. Another alternative is to view each program or event independently. An event that is focused on outreach into the community may be one where expenses are totally absorbed into the church/education budget. On the other hand, registration for a ski trip would likely be paid by each individual. Since it is important to be inclusive, some form of scholarship for those unable to afford the cost should be offered for any event that the church sponsors. It is a good idea to include a clause of confidentiality for anyone receiving the scholarships. This sometimes makes a difference in whether someone will make use of the offer. These scholarships may be full or partial, and they may also involve some sort of service. Many youth programs plan fund-raising events for their trips, and the youth then have a reduction of the registration fee depending on their amount of participation in the fund-raising events.

If the registration fee for a program is hefty, arrange for payment to be made over a period of several months, requiring that each installment be made by a certain time. This eases the financial burden on families and avoids last minute cancellations because people were unable to pay the amount. It forces you to plan ahead and makes sure that the family has set that time aside on their calendar.

Sunday School Offerings

In England, during the 1700s and 1800s most of the academic schools were either run by the churches or at least offered some religious training because the church and state were not separate entities. Sunday school was originally established as a mission outreach to the children who could not attend a regular school because they worked six days a week. The primary focus was to teach reading, writing, and arithmetic basics, although much of their reading was done with the Bible as their text. In the United States where the church

was declared separate from the state and after child labor laws were passed and enforced, Sunday school shifted toward religious education. It was also broadened to include all ages. However, for many years it continued to be operated as a separate entity from the church, completely run by laypeople. Often the pastor had no connection with the Sunday school, and the budget definitely was separate from the church. Most churches now recognize the importance of this educational program and underwrite the basic expenses of a Sunday school. However, it is important to use our giving in Sunday school as a tool for teaching stewardship to children and youth and as opportunities for adult classes to support the educational program.

In children's classes the offering is often treated in one of two ways. Either a basket is placed beside the door where children drop their money in and likely think it's a "gate entrance fee," or the offering is collected at the beginning of the session with no connection to the theme of the lesson. This usually occurs because of convenience. Generally, it is easier for those collecting the money from the classes to do so early in the session. However, it negates the real reason for an offering. The following are two ways to enrich the meaning of the offering for the children and youth.

• Look at the membership vows of your church and establish a place near the door of each classroom to help children and youth recognize ways that we fulfill those vows, including our monetary gifts. This might include a place to:

• In order to take up the offering at the time in the session when it is meaningful to the lesson (as a true offering of self, after preparing for this through study), a class may choose to save the offering from one week's session and have it ready to be placed in the class envelope at the beginning of the next class time, then saving that week's offering for the next session, and so forth. This way the offering becomes an interwoven part of the lesson but there is regular contribution from the class.

Adult classes need to realize that their giving helps to supplement the children's giving. Even if an adult class does not depend on the church budget to purchase curriculum, it is important for them to recognize their support to the purchase of the children's curriculum. Someone supported them when they were children, and they should reciprocate the gesture. In addition, adult classes may select to reserve a certain percentage of their regular offering for a class mission project. This is important because such mission projects help to build community and purpose in the class. The amount reserved for such projects will depend on the amount of money needed by such endeavors. If this procedure is followed, be sure that the class members are frequently reminded of the various ways their money is used, including the monetary support of the younger classes.

Most churches, however, find it more expedient to simply classify the Sunday school offering as income in the general budget and then provide curriculum and supplies for Sunday school from the budget of the education program. This process eliminates the need for a separate cash-flow account.

Activity	Accompanying Sign
List someone for whom the class may pray	*We support our church with our prayers.*
Register attendance	*We support our church with our presence.*
Place offering	*We support our church with our gifts.*
List or draw a picture of something a student has done for someone else during the week	*We support our church with our service.*

Fund-Raiser Friday Night

Fund-Raising Pros and Cons

As you will see in chapter 6, our understanding of giving and stewardship has gone through a variety of changes over the two thousand years of Christianity. In this new millennium we must recognize the individual rights for persons to choose where they see God directing them to give their gifts. Therefore it is important to communicate the missional aspects of any program for which you are raising funds.

Much has already been written about fund-raising. However, it is important to recognize just why we have fund-raisers and to think through whether it is appropriate in each situation. Perhaps this can best be done by simply listing some pros and cons for fund-raising:

Pro	Con
Increased visibility of project	Negative feeling by those "hit for the money"
Community building	Competition for funds can be negative
Gives ownership on part of participant	Consumes much time and energy
Involves congregation if recognized as a mission of entire church	Takes ownership away from congregation if fund-raisers consider it "my project"

The primary consideration in fund-raising is not the end result of raising enough funds, but rather the mission that such a project accomplishes. This should be kept as the central focus.

One church began raising funds for a youth mission project by spending a Sunday in mission to the congregation. During the morning the youth cleaned the windshields of all of the cars in the parking lot. On each windshield they left a note that explained that they were preparing for their mission trip by being in mission to the members of the congregation. They did not ask for money, but because of this outreach to the congregation, there was a better attitude about the mission on the part of the participants as well as the members of the congregation. Later, when they sold "shares" in the mission trip, there was a favorable response. Upon their return, the youth prepared a supper for the shareholders and gave a detailed report of their experience and insights.

Although we want fund-raising to be enjoyable for the participants, other members should not be made to feel guilty if this is not a project they feel called to support. Help those working to raise funds to realize that everyone does not need to support every project. Congregations can sometimes turn potential members away because the church is perceived as a money-grabbing institution.

Basic Supplies and Supply Rooms

Depending on your personality traits, supplies and supply rooms can be the least of your worries or a major bone of contention. Nonetheless, these areas are often in need of attention. Do not, however, assume responsibility for organizing the supply room yourself. It will eat up all of your time. This is one temptation that I must resist because I do enjoy order and seeing everything in its place, although my study does not show this personality trait! I've learned the law that "Work expands to fill the time allotted to it." In order to have things arranged orderly in a supply room that everyone accesses, a significant amount of time is required. So I locate a volunteer who will take ownership of this ministry of providing teachers and other volunteers with the supplies that they need. It is one of the behind-the-scenes jobs that seldom gets the affirmation and recognition that it deserves.

My most successful recruitment for a volunteer to fill this position occurred after placing an "ad" in the bulletin saying, "Are you the type of person who likes to see things in their proper place? Do you enjoy organizing and arranging things? Then we have a real ministry for you!" A church member read the announcement and discovered that her calling was not teaching, but rather organization of supplies.

She set our supply room in order, purchased supplies when needed, and assisted teachers in their preparation for their classes. She was much happier in this ministry, and her talents gifted the teachers with a much calmer classroom, because they had what they needed and knew where to find it.

Some churches enter into a debate about whose supplies are whose, locking supply closets and doling out the materials only to "those qualified" to receive them. This only creates division in the church, something that Jesus certainly challenged in his ministry. An open supply room for all groups in the church usually works best. When planning the budget, simply anticipate that all groups in the church program will have access to the supplies and that the money for supplies will be provided with that understanding. If the physical facility is large, you may need to provide several substations for basic supplies for teachers in a specific area. However, the central supply "depot" should handle the purchasing and disbursing of all supplies.

One other thing is important about budgets and supplies. Communicate clearly to teachers and volunteers that they are not expected to purchase their own supplies. However, if occasionally they must purchase something, they should expect reimbursement. Teachers sometimes say, "Oh, that's just my contribution." Discourage this practice since it is important for you to know how much is being spent in order to budget effectively in the coming year. They also need to realize that someone else may not be able to afford such a contribution and might decline from teaching because of an inability to purchase supplies.

Here is a general list of basic supplies that you will want to include. If your budget does not allow you to purchase these right away, consider a "Supply Shower." Set a date and ask everyone in the church to bring an item from the list to help fill your supply closet. Decorate several reception centers with umbrellas and flowers, using the theme of *Showers Bringing Forth Blooms in Christian Education.*

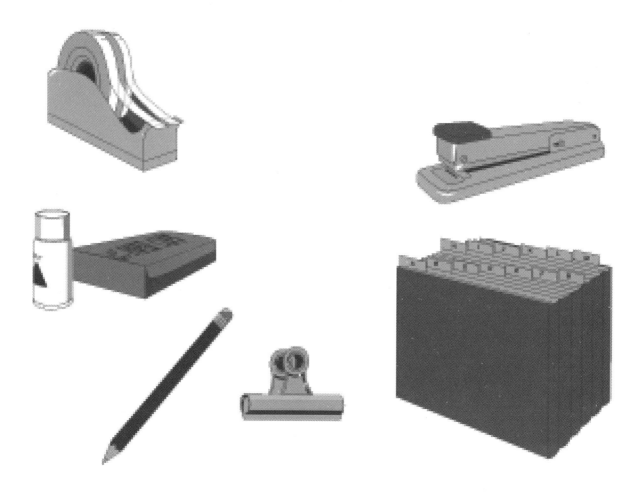

The Nuts & Bolts of Christian Education

Each classroom should have:

- ❏ writing and drawing paper,
- ❏ pencils,
- ❏ markers,
- ❏ crayons,
- ❏ staplers, staples,
- ❏ tape (transparent and masking)

- ❏ glue, glue sticks,
- ❏ scissors (round-nose, left-handed, pointed),
- ❏ rulers,
- ❏ chalk and eraser,
- ❏ bulletin board tacks or pins.

Besides replacement supplies for the classroom, the supply room may also include:

- ❏ beads, buttons, and sequins
- ❏ Bible story pictures
- ❏ Bible translations
- ❏ biblical costumes
- ❏ boxes and cartons
- ❏ brads
- ❏ candles and matches
- ❏ cloth scraps
- ❏ clothes pins (straight and snap)
- ❏ construction paper (mostly 9" x 12" and some 12" x 18")
- ❏ contact paper (clear)
- ❏ cotton balls
- ❏ craft sticks (for stirring paint and spreading glue, as well as for crafts)
- ❏ dishwashing liquid (add a little to paints for easier cleanup)
- ❏ egg cartons
- ❏ electric frying pan (for heating wax in cans, placed in water)
- ❏ felt fabric and squares
- ❏ finger-painting paper (glossy shelf paper works)
- ❏ fixative spray
- ❏ glitter
- ❏ greeting cards
- ❏ hammers and nails
- ❏ hole punch
- ❏ iron and small ironing board
- ❏ liquid starch (to add to water-base paint for finger paint)
- ❏ magazines for cutting

- ❏ maps
- ❏ molding clay and play dough
- ❏ nature articles such as feathers, pine cones, shells, etc.
- ❏ newspapers
- ❏ newsprint or large paper
- ❏ paint (powdered is cheaper, in many colors)
- ❏ paint shirts (men's old shirts worn backward)
- ❏ paintbrushes
- ❏ paint-mixing bowls or covered jars for mixing paint
- ❏ paper clips
- ❏ paper cups and plates
- ❏ paper (plain and lined)
- ❏ pins (safety and straight)
- ❏ plastic bags (many sizes)
- ❏ plastic sheets or other floor protection
- ❏ poster board in variety of colors
- ❏ rolls of wax paper, aluminum foil, etc.
- ❏ rubber cement
- ❏ sewing notions (lace, trim, etc.)
- ❏ stickers
- ❏ string
- ❏ tissues
- ❏ tubes from paper towels and bathroom tissue
- ❏ wallpaper sample books
- ❏ wash pans (if no sinks in rooms)
- ❏ watercolor paint sets
- ❏ yardstick
- ❏ yarn

There will be additional supplies that you will also find helpful. Be sure to include a first-aid kit in the supply room and at other central locations around the facility.

Finally, always consider good stewardship when using supplies. Avoid using food for crafts. If we tell children that people are starving and then use food for crafts, we are giving mixed signals. Provide a box for bits and pieces of construction paper that can be used again. Recycle paper by using both sides. Avoid use of Styrofoam and other materials that are not environment-friendly.

Electronic and Other Equipment for Classroom and General Use

Electronic equipment is becoming more affordable and changing so rapidly that many churches have a variety of equipment at their disposal. Most curriculum now offers audiotapes or compact disks to enrich the teaching experience. There are also videos that make a good basis for class discussion.

Each classroom will benefit from having a tape player and/or CD player in the room. Encourage teachers to use these for gathering music as well as for appointed times during the session. Tape familiar songs as they are being sung by your congregation so young learners can sing along with them, learning the words as they work. If the tape/CD player is portable, it can be taken to other locations with the class. Basic tape players can be used at preschool learning centers by placing red and green stickers on the start and stop buttons.

Some teachers, particularly leaders of adults, appreciate an overhead projector. If this is on a movable cart, the transparencies and pens can be stored on the cart. Also useful are display easels for newsprint pads, along with markers. When these are used, the printed sheets may be displayed on the walls of the classroom. Check to be sure that it is permissible to use tape on your walls; sometimes a strip of cork along the walls is provided for displays.

Every church needs a television and VCR on a moveable stand. This can be stored in a locked closet or media room when not in use, but be sure that it is easily available to the classrooms. If your facility is large, you will want to have several in accessible locations. Post a use chart for teachers to reserve the use of the VCR. A collection of commercial videotapes can be kept with the equipment or in your church library so that families can borrow them for home use.

Computer software for Christian education is becoming more readily available. See page 18 concerning computers and computer labs.

Access to a copy machine is very valuable. Encourage teachers to request or make copies early in the week so that they are finished and available when needed in the classroom.

A slide projector and carousels are still useful. Slides can be made by bleaching old negative strips, drawing on them with fine-line permanent markers, and mounting them in empty slide frames.

Cameras offer many creative learning opportunities. A simple print camera can even be used by preschoolers with the assistance of an adult. With a video camera a class can produce and record a biblical drama to share with another class or with the whole church. The digital cameras offer great publishing options because the disk can be used immediately in a computer. They are certainly worth considering if your church has a large film developing bill because the disk can be used repeatedly. Pictures that are not wanted can be deleted, while others can be stored on a computer hard drive or removable disk.

Classes, Classrooms, and Curriculum

As the person in primary leadership of Christian education in your church, you will want to be knowledgeable about the classes being offered, as well as the classrooms and curriculum being used. As you go about your work do not take the "Last Seven Words in the Church" (We have always done it that way.) as the way it should be! Use the information you find within these pages, and then do more research as needed. It is important for your ministry and educational program that you feel confident in your knowledge.

Classes

Some church leaders may have an idealistic picture of children's church school as a large group of small children sitting around a table enthralled by their teacher. Indeed publishers, for many years, affirmed this attitude by picturing children's classes like this in their curriculum. However, realistically,

we all learn best by participation, and children learn best by participating physically. Add movement to children's short attention spans and large classes become bedlam. Therefore it is important to create new classes when one becomes too large.

It is sad, but we live in a litigious society and so we must legally protect ourselves by always having two adults in a classroom with children and youth. This arrangement protects teachers from accusations of abuse since another adult is always present. Consider using parents and senior adults on a rotating basis to help in the classroom simply as loving arms, assisting with activities, and sitting among the children during group time. Some churches require that parents take a turn in the classroom, not teaching but simply being on hand to assist. For more suggestions on staffing the classrooms see pages 55-56 in chapter 7. The following are general suggestions for the teacher/student ratio within a classroom:

- 3 infants and creepers per adult (with additional on-call persons in fire emergency—see page 35 and appendix 12)
- 6 toddlers per adult
- 8 preschoolers per adult
- 10 kindergartners per adult
- 12 six- to eight-year-olds per adult
- 14 nine-year-olds or older per adult (including senior highs)

Class Registration

No matter what the size of your Sunday school program, it is important to keep an accurate registration of the students and classes. Advance registration also helps as you staff your teaching team. Typically, I designate several Sundays in the spring as registration days. During those Sundays tables are set up at central locations where parents stop and register their children for all summer events and for classes for the next fall. The children continue in their current classes until fall, but this system allows adequate time during the summer months to assign classes, and for teachers to write welcome notes to their students, reminding them of the new class year.

Parents appreciate being able to fill out one registration form for the entire family, such as the sample in appendix 11, rather than a separate form for each student.

The best procedure for dealing with visitors and new students is to have a central Sunday school office where all new students are directed. The visitors are greeted, informed of the program (with a well-written printed piece, including adult class information), asked to fill out a registration form, and then assigned classes. I prefer to have registration forms filled out even for visitors. This provides us with information on parents, addresses, and so forth.

If more than one class for a specific age is offered, you will find that during the year the classes will become uneven in number. This occurs when visiting parents simply drop off their children in the most conveniently located classroom when they first arrive at church. The best way to avoid this imbalance is to have all teachers ask visiting and new families to go to the Sunday school office first.

Workshop Rotation Model

Children's Sunday school classes can be organized in a variety of ways. *The Workshop Rotation Model* uses several workshops through which the classes rotate. Each workshop features a particular method, such as *art, drama, Bible skills and games, video,* and *computer* to get a particular story or theme across to students. The lead teacher in each workshop adjusts the teaching method according to the age of the children in the class in that workshop on that particular week. Naturally there must be adjustments to the regular curriculum, and a knowledgeable team of planners is a necessity. Curriculum is available that has been written specifically for this model. Contact Cokesbury or contact Neil MacQueen at 800-678-1948 or visit his Web site www.rotation.com.

This model of classes works best if you have at least one teacher who is consistently with the same class no matter which workshop they attend. Additional helpers may be brought in for each workshop, depending on what is needed for that week.

Dual Sessions

I once worked in a large, growing church where we faced a real dilemma. Our classes were outgrowing our space; and although there were plans for a new building, a solution needed to be found immediately. The solution we used was to implement dual sessions of Sunday school and an additional worship hour. If your church is considering dual sessions, the following suggestions may be helpful.
Before making the decision:
• Take a tour of your church to determine if all spaces are being used.
• Can some classes and classrooms be shuffled for better accommodation?
• Can some space now being used for other things be adapted to Sunday school?
• Will minor remodeling help? Remember that adult classes do not feel so crowded if there are two doors to their room, allowing better access.
• Is adjacent space available? (for example, school building, bank building, and so forth.)
• Consider portable classrooms.
• Look at your overcrowding on paper, room by room. This should include recommended capacity for existing floor space (see pages 33-34), average attendance in past years, highest attendance in past years, and numbers of adult members not listed on any class rolls.
As you develop your plan consider:
• How will you determine who attends which session?
• How are you planning for the multiple use of rooms (room arrangement, use of supplies, turnaround time, teacher training, bulletin boards, and so forth)?
• What provisions have been made for the registration and placement of new people?
• How will children and youth choir performances and schedules affect Sunday school classes and the morning schedule?
• What alternative times, spaces, and days have you considered? What are the pros and cons to each alternative?
• What are the special needs of your congregation and community that should be taken into account?

DUAL SESSIONS

• How does your schedule honor the educational and worship needs of children? youth? adults? families (two-parent and single)? Single adults?

• What are your plans for transition time? (for example, members entering and leaving, cleanup and setup, parking, and so forth)

• How do you plan to integrate special services, such as confirmation or presentation of Bibles, into worship services?

• How will this schedule affect any Sunday morning confirmation classes?

As individuals and families consider their schedule, have them ask such questions as:

• Do you enjoy coming early and having the remainder of the day for other activities, or do you enjoy sleeping late and using the later hours for church?

• Are your children early risers, and would the two early hours (such as 8:30 and 10:00 A.M.) be better for them when they are not restless?

• Do you go out for lunch after church, and how would a schedule change affect your routine?

• How would a schedule change affect your Sunday schedule?

Make every effort to encourage families to attend Sunday school and worship together. However,

there should be something for everyone at both hours. Although you will encourage children to attend worship, having dual sessions will naturally attract some new parents who want to put their children in Sunday school while they attend worship. Recognize that this may increase your children's classes. Realize that a dual session will not relieve your space situation in the preschool room. In fact, it may complicate it. You will continue to have children with you for two hours who normally attend a nursery during the church service.

In planning room assignments, try to avoid moving young children from one classroom to another. Stability is important, and young children may be fearful that parents cannot find them. If you must move children, it is better to accomplish the move with your teaching/nursery staff rather than asking parents to come between their class and worship to move them. Be sure that parents know where to pick up their children.

Be aware that the youth classes at the new hour are sometimes the hardest to establish. If the class is small, look for curriculum with a wide age span. Select popular teachers for the new hour who will draw students to the class. Look for youth who enjoy small group discussions, and center the class or classes on this style of teaching. These youth may be moving into the inquiring or searching style of faith and need opportunities for deeper study. Be certain that teachers of such a group are *clarifiers* of the faith, who stand on neutral ground and can help students think through their questions to find their own answers. Inquiring students appreciate help in knowing *how* to think, not being told *what* to think. Consider asking youth who enjoy being together, to commit to attending a specific class for a year. You might even consider asking for "family commitments" from the adults, children, and youth in the same family (where they agree to attend their classes for one year to help establish the classes). Finally, teenagers enjoy meeting for juice and doughnuts between the two class hours. This gives them an opportunity to visit with each other even if they attend different classes.

If adult classes are not provided during both sessions, some parents will place their children in Sunday school while they attend worship. When this happens, the children miss worship and the adults miss study. Try to keep current adult classes intact, moving some to the new hour as well as adding new classes. (*Leading Adult Learners* offers help here.) A new class formed around a specific subject can later become an ongoing class. This is also a good time to initiate perspective member and teacher training classes. Another option for adults is a family class. (See page 12 for more information about family classes.)

A large class may choose to divide into two groups that meet at separate hours, but gather between the two class hours for fellowship time. Advise parents to pick up their children before they fellowship so that teachers are not late to their next hour's commitment. In addition, ask that parents choose to attend one class hour and stick with it so that their children have consistency in their class. It is important that children's classes build unity.

Regardless of the options offered, be certain that there is a balance of adult classes in both hours. Work to achieve this balance by considering:

- Ages of the children in the families (and/or ages of the adult class members)
- Larger and small classes (where possible)
- Discussion and lecture format
- Bible study with relation to everyday life or contemporary issues with biblical references
- Assigned teacher or rotating leaders among class members

Here are a few other points to consider. One person will need to coordinate the whole Sunday school experience, either laity or staff. If a layperson is selected, then the staff person is available to move about the classes and evaluate the situation better. There is also a plus for the staff person to spend a Sunday here and there teaching a few of the adult classes. It's a good idea to choose a director for each hour, who will be available in the Sunday school office for guidance and emergency decisions.

Remember to select a Sunday school clerk (or whoever collects the money and records the total attendance) for each session. Age-level coordinators can be handled in two ways. Either have one overall coordinator with an assistant to handle the on-the-spot work at the other hour, or select two coordinators for each age level (one for each hour). The advantage in having a coordinator with an assistant is that one person sees the whole picture for an entire

age level. The coordinator will also, hopefully, be aware of the needs of an age group and how those needs are being met at times other than Sunday morning.

Classrooms

I visited a church that had added an educational building the previous year. The size of the rooms were perfect, and each held chalkboards, as well as chairs and tables of the proper height. But when I walked up to the door I had no desire to go inside, since I could see nothing besides tables and chairs. I followed my friend into the room, and then turned around to find a great display that reflected the theme of the study. That experience helped me understand how a student might feel when approaching the room for the first time. The classroom is the first impression that students have about their classes. They may not always be ideal in size, but there are usually simple ways that can improve the atmosphere and friendliness of a classroom. Review the age level characteristics in appendix 2 and then ask the following questions as you evaluate a classroom:

- As you approach the room, how can you tell who meets here?
- As you enter the room, stand or squat at the eye level of the students who meet here. What do you see? Is there something that would make you (as a visitor) want to come into the room? What? Is the room light? dark? Are there bright colors in the room?
- What in the room gives a hint of the subject for this Sunday?
- Is there anything outdated that is still in the room? What?

- Is the room accessible for persons with physical disabilities?
- Is the furniture the appropriate size? Is there too much furniture? Can the furniture be better arranged to allow space for active learning?

It is important for all children and youth classrooms to have a window in the door, so as to avoid potential legal pitfalls. This practice is highly recommended by Joy Melton in her book, *Safe Sanctuaries: Reducing the Risk of Child Abuse in the Church* (see Resources and References) and is actually helpful to administrators as it solves possible legal problems.

At some point you are likely to need to plan for new classrooms or changes in the locations of some classes. Church planning teams often operate under the mistaken belief that smaller people equal smaller furniture equal smaller space. The first two parts of this equation are true, but the third is false. In fact, the opposite is actually true. The smaller the child (except for children under six months) the more space required. Listed below are guidelines to consider when planning for different ages.

The general recommendation for space for preschool age is thirty-five square feet per child, with forty square feet when play equipment is in the room. Classrooms that will be used for weekday preschool activities will usually have equipment.

The ideal plan for *infants and creepers* is to have two connected rooms, one for sleeping and one for when children are awake. Children would be brought in and taken out through the waking room. It is also important to have hallway space outside the door to alleviate crowding when parents drop off and pick up their children. Bed space, rocking chairs, floor space for crawlers, and room for adult workers must be considered in these rooms. It is important to have divided doors for receiving the child. This type of door has a top half that opens separately and has a shelf attached to the bottom half. The arrangement provides less confusion when parents are leaving and picking up children; when the child does not see other adults entering and leaving the room, he or she is not as anxious about the parent's return. Infant and creeper rooms need sink facilities for washing hands and cleaning up after changing dirty diapers, spit-ups, and so forth. Hot water is also needed for heating bottles. The floors should be carpeted, and a clean sheet may be placed over the carpet for babies to roll on. Some churches run heat pipes below the surface of the floor in creeper rooms to provide warmth in the winter.

Toddlers and two-year-olds characteristically participate in parallel play, playing alone with toys, near another child. Crowding causes children to intrude on each other's privacy, resulting in frustration and frequent fights. Often, this is the first exposure that this age-level child has to the church, and it may be the first experience of play with more than two or three children in a room. Hopefully, this is a positive experience for the child, and therefore a positive experience for their parents. Horizontally divided doors are a plus for this room so that the child is handed to the parent without opening the lower half. Divided doors also avoid the problem of a child slipping out of the room as the door is opened. It is important for this room to be well lit and to have outside windows at the child's level. A child-size bathroom, connected to another preschool room, is ideal for this age. Water is certainly necessary for diaper and accident cleanups. A carpet that withstands scrubbing is good for this room, although part of the floor may be tiled for messy projects.

Threes, fours, and kindergarten-age children learn best through experiential methods of teaching, and this requires floor as well as table space. There should be room for centers where children can pretend housekeeping and play with blocks, as well as room for total group activity away from the tables. The floor should be tiled and carpeted. The carpeted area can be used for the block center and as the group activity space. These rooms need connecting bathrooms so that children may use them without a teacher having to leave the classroom to take a child to the restroom. It is important to have built-in cabinets with enough storage for Sunday morning and weekday materials, and sinks of child height in the classrooms for cleanups after such activities as pasting and painting.

The recommended space for *elementary* age children is thirty square feet per child. Proper teaching of this age involves experiential activities. This means that floor space as well as table space is important. Bathrooms need to be nearby but not necessarily connecting. There should be a carpeted area for sitting together either on chairs or on the floor.

The required space for *youth* is twenty-five square feet each. Both middle school and senior high students need to be in small groupings at times during their sessions, and so furniture should be easy to move around. Youth learn through talking with each other about the subject, not by simply sitting and listening to a lecture. They are entering the inquiring or searching style of faith, and it is important that they have opportunities for small-group discussions about what they are learning. At least one of the youth rooms needs to have casual furniture, such as sofa and chairs. These rooms need to be bright with plenty of wall space for hanging posters, and so forth.

Adults require twenty square feet per person. Learners in adult classes do not feel as crowded if there are windows and two doors in the classroom As you plan, consider that at gathering and dismissing times adults tend to linger around the doors, causing congestion. According to studies, most classes of larger than twenty-five to thirty people cannot function well in any format other than lecture. No matter what the format, it is certainly preferable for chairs to be placed in a semicircle or circle rather than in straight rows. This allows adults to see each other and to develop relationships within the group. Dividing a large class into small groups is an option, but requires additional space. In a large group, when discussion is used, certain members may attempt to dominate the conversation. Others who may want to speak but are a little hesitant may feel ignored or that their statements are unimportant, and so they do not make the effort. Smaller groups help to alleviate both of these problems.

The coffee or visiting time before the learning experience is important for adults. A built-in cabinet for storage and counter space with a small sink is desirable in each adult classroom. If the sink is not available, then a nearby water source is important.

Throughout the building it is important to have "gathering areas" near the outside doors so conversations do not cause hallway congestion.

Finding Space

But, you say, we just don't have the space for additional classes. You may be surprised where classes can meet. I worked for two years with a facility where we only had a room for a nursery (which doubled as my office during the week) and the fellowship hall for children's classes on Sunday morning. Because of the lack of space we held the primary educational program on a weekday afternoon when we could use the sanctuary, choir room, and pastor's study. However we did have classes through the third grade on Sunday. Three-year-olds through third grade met in the fellowship hall, divided by portable chalk boards and large refrigerator boxes. Split open and flattened, these refrigerator boxes stood by themselves. Then they could be folded for storage when not in use.

When I was a volunteer teacher in a smaller church, I taught a first-through-third-grade class behind the piano in the one-room church building. In another church we held Sunday school class in the kitchen, while in another we often met outside under the trees because our classroom was so small.

Take a tour of the building. Are the rooms being used to their best advantage? Has an older class dwindled but been reluctant to relinquish the room because of tradition?

Wherever possible, establish a policy that no class has ownership of a room, thereby allowing you to practice good stewardship of your space. If you are moving into a new building, consider converting to a system of using room numbers instead of class names when you refer to a room. This helps to center class ownership on the persons in the class instead of on a specific classroom.

Emergency/Fire Plan

One night I awoke, terrified about a dream. The church where I was working had the children's classrooms in a half-basement. In many of the classrooms the windows were of old stained glass. I dreamed that there was a fire, and the children were trying to break the stained glass in order to get out. I realized that we had no emergency or fire evacuation plan for our over-crowded classrooms.

If you are without a plan for evacuation in the event of an emergency or fire, use appendix 12 to design one. If you already have a plan in place, use the form to review its completeness.

Shared Space

At some point, you may need to help resolve a dispute between two groups that share a space in the facility. Frequently, this situation occurs between Sunday school teachers and a weekday program. If possible, work out potential difficulties early on, before they cause a problem.

It is best to get everything down in a printed shared-space agreement so that all arrangements for space use are clear. As you plan your meeting of both groups, consider these things:

• How can you create a pleasant and comfortable atmosphere for the meeting? Should it be over a meal? Round tables or seating in a circle make for better communication.

• What is the understanding of stewardship (not just finances) behind shared space and how can this be conveyed to the users?

• Are you removed enough from all sides to act as mediator, or should you invite someone else in?

• Who is involved in using this space? (include groups such as Scout troops, parent groups, and so forth)

• Does your church consider other groups using the space as an outreach or mission to the community? This will make a difference in whether there is a charge and how much. If the church, for instance, picks up some of the facility expenses for a preschool, then there is less cost for the student.

• How can you create a worshipful atmosphere as you make this agreement, and how can the final agreement be acknowledged by prayer or a consecration?

Here are some items to consider as you work through your agreements:

• Where can you have a communications center (such as a bulletin board) that deals specifically with shared space?

• How can you help the leaders who will be using shared space become better acquainted so that problems can be worked out on a friendly basis?

• What time agreements need to be worked through? (Identify the days and time needed for all those using the space—include preparation time for all parties.)

• What space agreements need to be worked through? (More space may be added as you design the agreement. Besides rooms, include fellowship hall, gymnasium, restrooms, playground, hallways, parking lot spaces, exits and entrances, and kitchen. Check for any licensing requirements, particularly about kitchens, as they may exclude sharing food preparation spaces and restrooms while one group is in session.)

• What rules will be enforced by all parties so that there is consistency, safety, and understanding? (Consider rules such as no running in halls, an agreed-on degree of noise, no sitting on tables, keeping sand in sandbox, big wheel toys used only in designated area, equipment stored in locked area after use, and so forth.)

• Which leaders will be responsible for what in the classrooms? (such as checking on supplies needed, paint materials stored in air tight containers, and so forth)

• What space in the classroom is assigned to each group exclusively? (bulletin boards, storage space, exposed work areas, and so forth)

• What supplies in a classroom are shared and what will be done with those not shared when the group is not using the room? (such as books, toys, scissors, crayons, paper, glue, paint brushes, and so forth)

• What costs need to be shared?

—Will a group pay usage fee? How will it be assessed? (by square footage, percentage of income, and so forth)

—How will you share cost of utilities such as housekeeping service, telephone, janitorial supplies, heat and air, copy machine and other office equipment, postage, secretarial services?

—Who will pay for repair and replacement of equipment, such as playground equipment?

—Will all groups share in the insurance cost? Does it go up with additional use?

Once your agreement is in place, be sure that everyone involved has a copy and understands it thoroughly. Assign persons to carry out such requirements as posting the rules for the playground and/or kitchen, rearranging any storage or usage areas, seeing that each leader has the name and phone number of everyone else using the room for better communication, and other duties that will make your program run more smoothly.

Policy

In general, churches have many policies that they must deal with. It is important to be aware of what policies your church already has in place and be alert to others that may need to be added. A few are listed below:

• Pick-up procedures for children in nursery (Be aware that some churches have experienced problems with a noncustodial parent who picks up a child.)

• Advance notice to parents regarding activities

• Appropriate disciplining procedures

• Media/electronic equipment use

• Use of the van or bus (who has preference, reserving its use, age of driver, food or drink inside, loud music or noise that inhibits driver from hearing emergency vehicles, seat belts and remaining seated, refilling gas tank before returning, and so forth)

• Field trips/retreats (ratio of adults to children or youth, distance traveled, permission slips—see appendix 13)

• Two-adult rule (always having two adults in a classroom or with children or youth)

• Open-door counseling with children and youth

• Procedure and training for child abuse and for being aware of possible sexual abuse

• Background checks and screening process for workers/volunteers, including length of membership in a church before being asked to serve with children/youth

• Forms on file of all those working with children or youth

• Incidents of infectious diseases (including AIDS)

Achievement Goals

One of the hardest things to do is to measure the learning achievements of students. In fact, harder than that is to actually set the goals. If we are too strict about specific goals, we turn away those whom we really need to reach. For this reason, I caution against rewarding Bible verse memorization, attendance, and so forth. These of course need to be encouraged. But, particularly with children, these things are often out of their control. Many children spend several weekends a month with a parent other than the one they live with during the week. This causes erratic church attendance over which the children have no control.

Work with your education committee to develop goals for those who attend Sunday school on a regular basis. The goals of your church may be different from those of other churches because of the individuals in your church. For example, if your community is culturally mixed, you might move the culture goal to a younger age. As you develop your goals, refer to appendix 14, "Guidelines for Selecting Bible Stories," as well as the following suggestions categorized by age level.

Goals in Bible Skills, Prayer, Stewardship, and Mission

Ages 0-1   Experience a loving and safe atmosphere in the church.

Recognize the word *church* as an exciting place to be.

Recognize the words *God* and *Jesus* as important words at church and at home.

Hear simple prayers being said, such as "Thank you, God, for the food."

Use their exploratory nature to heighten self-appreciation. (Children cannot recognize and appreciate something different from themselves until they know themselves.)

Enjoy parallel play, growing in appreciation of others.

Ages 2-3   Recognize that favorite stories come from the Bible and the Bible is important to us.

Learn that the Bible tells us about God and Jesus.

Use markers to find simple verses and stories in the Bible.

Associate prayer with good things.

Hear simple language in prayers, such as "you" and "your" instead of "thee" and "thou."

Pray five-to six-word prayers after adults.

Hear praise for their positive actions, helping to set a loving attitude.

Have the opportunity to play with items such as dolls with various racial traits and dress-up clothes from many cultures, giving them subtle suggestions of ethnic and cultural differences.

Ages 4-5   Be able to retell some of their favorite Bible stories.

Have some opportunities for prayer, leading to spontaneous "talking" prayers to God.

Learn games, songs, and stories from other cultures. (They will not understand the cultural difference, but they will experience a game that they will later learn is from another culture.)

Learn an occasional word for names and numbers in other languages.

Come to know persons from different cultures who have positive attitudes.

Use new skills in group activity to develop a sense of belonging and love for one another.

Serve with persons of other ages in order to develop a growing sense of pride in the church family and recognition of ways the church helps others.

Experience service to others in order to realize that persons in the church family come together to study and worship God, and then go out to serve.

Find simple ways to use their talents and abilities to help others.

Grades 1-3   Learn that the Old Testament was written before the time of Jesus and contains scripture he read.

Learn that the New Testament tells about Jesus and those who spread the message of Jesus after his death and resurrection.

Learn about customs, dress, and food of Bible days.

Continue with prayers of praise and thanksgiving.

Create litany prayers together.

Compose some written prayers.

Begin prayers asking God for help.

Have opportunities for sentence prayers *after* discussion of what we are thankful for.

Have opportunities to meet people from different cultures, recognizing that there are many ways of doing things.

Have expanded opportunities for songs, games, and stories from other cultures.

Grow in accepting responsibility of own actions and acknowledging need for forgiveness.

Begin to look at situations from different

viewpoints, think about how others feel in given positions.

Grade 1: Become familiar with some of the names of the books of the Bible and persons in Bible. By the end of the year, begin to learn names of the Gospels and that *gospel* means "Good News."

Grade 2: Read small sections from the Bible and learn key words.

Become familiar with the Bible's table of contents.

Use bookmarks that the teacher has placed in the Bible ahead of time.

Grade 3: Begin to associate books with sections of Bible (Proverbs = Wisdom; Romans = Letters, and so forth)

Learn beginning Bible skills: book, chapter, verse, abbreviation of books.

Grades 4-6 Learn to use a children's Bible dictionary

Frequently practice skills of locating scripture passages.

Locate the books of the Bible according to category.

Use maps with Bible study.

Learn about the historical development of the Bible.

Memorize the names of the books of the Bible.

Develop a growing understanding of prayer as an important way we relate to God.

Use personal devotional material.

Study some of the formal prayers and creeds of the church and appreciate their heritage.

Study prayers for special occasions that are found in the hymnal.

Recognize that there are many ways to worship.

As understanding of geography develops, recognize how Christians around the world tell and show others what God has done. Be introduced to the word *witness*.

Begin to see themselves in the eyes of others.

Experience "standing in the moccasins of others."

Develop appreciation of God's concern for all people.

Become aware of ways Christians respond to God's love through missions.

Grow in management of their personal time and recognize themselves as stewards of their time, learning to use time wisely.

Learn that money is of God's creation and belongs to God. Learn to recognize money as a result of the way we use our talents.

Grow in appreciation of the way that our money functions in the church, including financial necessities to maintain the church.

Be introduced to tithing.

Expand understanding of service for others through the church by acting in mission as a class and individually.

Be involved in regular responsibilities in the church.

Grades 7-8 Compare different Gospel writers' versions of the same story.

Use footnotes/cross-references in the Bible.

Begin journaling experiences.

Continue growth in private devotions.

Learn about the persons of our heritage who wrote some of the prayers and creeds of the church.

Begin to use intercessory prayers in class.

Recognize that prayers will help them through difficult situations.

Learn to distinguish between independence and interdependence, recognizing that everyone must work together for justice. (Matthew 20:1-16)

Grow in understanding of the difference between *justice* and *fair*. (In justice, everyone has the right to basic needs such as life, food, shelter, education, employment, proper medical care, clean water and air, security of body and emotions, and the opportunity to direct and govern themselves.)

Use research and conversational skills to

find out about everyday life and celebrations in other cultures.

Have opportunities for mission trips.

Senior High Use concordance to locate references on a specific theme.

Recognize greater importance of prayer in personal life.

Continue intercessory prayer.

Have more pointed experiences with journaling.

Develop specific skills and talents that can be used as stewards.

Grow in understanding of tithing.

Become more involved with extended mission trips.

Become more involved in leadership in the church, including serving on committees.

Become familiar with Bible translations (versions that observe strict scholarly rules and stay close to the original text) and paraphrases (versions that freely add interpretative materials to the original text).

Use commentaries.

Experience intensive Bible study.

Curriculum

Often the printed resources that are used in the church are referred to as the *curriculum* when in reality the whole design or plan for the education program is the curriculum; the printed material is only a part of the curriculum resources. These printed materials usually come in two forms, *dated* and *undated*. The dated curriculum is intended to be used on a certain date and is available for a limited time. Undated curriculum, sometimes called electives, are available indefinitely and may be used at almost any time of the year. Usually undated curriculum is planned for use over a four- to six-week period, but sometimes the time frame extends to a full year.

Many of the adult classes prefer the undated resources because they can select their subject of study. Undated material can also be used for youth, but it is important to be sure that through the course of middle school and high school a good balance of Bible study and current issue studies is offered. Youth are focused on what's happening in their life, and so the Bible study even needs to have an emphasis on application to their lives.

Generally youth and adult resources fall into two categories: those that study a specific section of the Bible and apply that to life situations and those that lift up life situations and then apply biblical teachings to them. In addition, Bible study that is strictly centered on the Bible and has no application to our lives today is available. Such studies may not interest many young adults.

When considering curriculum (the whole plan for teaching including materials and methods) whether for children, youth, or adults, think about whether it will be *informational* or *formational*. Informational curriculum dwells on presentation of the materials and the learner primarily feeds back the information. Formational curriculum gives background information, but helps learners think through how the materials apply to their lives and involves much interaction between the learners. Moreover, informational curriculum often tells people "what to think" whereas formational helps them know "how to think" and encourages them to think on their own.

I recommend including a "Bible 101" course for adults each year in your church. This is a basic introductory course that gives lots of Bible background and even opportunity to practice finding passages in the Bible.

In selecting the materials, first and foremost recognize the policy, or establish a policy, that all curriculum materials should be approved by the education committee or board. Screen the materials first to save time, but it is helpful to have the approval of the committee if a complaint arises about resources that have been selected.

Second, explain the policy to teachers so that they understand why an overall plan for curriculum is desired instead of allowing each teacher to simply select material that appeals to them. The goal is for the learner to have a well-rounded learning experience, from beginning to end. Noah's ark is a delightful story and children like repetition, but there are other important stories in the Bible.

Third, become knowledgeable about your church's doctrinal views. Some denominations are strongly in favor of certain beliefs, while others leave the interpretation of everything other than basic beliefs up to the individual. If the material dogmatically pushes a belief that opposes your church or denominational view, then selection of that material does not do justice to your church or to your learners. Even if you personally agree with the belief, the material should leave the option open for each learner to explore.

Dated material printed or approved by your denomination generally falls into this category. However, there are also good materials that are not published by any specific denomination. If you do use them, recognize that you will need to supplement the material with information about your own denomination.

Here are several questions to ask when evaluating curriculum materials:

• How does the material carry out the purpose of Christian education in the denomination?

• How does the material help to fulfill the church's mission statement?

• How does the material help the learners to connect what they are learning with other aspects of the church, such as worship, stewardship, mission, and outreach?

• Does the material approach a variety of learning styles? (not just fill-in-the-blank and word puzzles)

• Does the material avoid racial and ethnic as well as male and female stereotypes?

• Does the material help the learners to connect what they are learning to their lives?

• Does the material encourage informational or formational teaching? (See above for explanation of these terms.)

• Am I letting the flashiness of the material convince me to use it without looking at the theology and age-level appropriateness?

Chapter 4

Decisions, Discovery, and Discernment

Decisions are often the root of our conflicts in the church. This is particularly true when change is involved. Often we do not deal with change effectively, usually because we find it threatening. The "old way" has become a part of us, and therefore we take any change from the norm as a threat to us personally. This often occurs when the people comprising a committee or board are from older and younger generations. Look at the generations summary in appendix 1. Notice that the young adults in Generation X and the Baby Boomers are questioning, flexible, and anxious to cut to the action without wasting time talking. They also have no strong dedication to one denomination or church, or to keeping things the way they are. On the other hand, older generations resist change, prefer consistent traditions, like to deliberate, and are slow to make decisions. No wonder we have difficulty within the governing body of our churches!

As a Christian, it is important to first seek God's will in a situation before making decisions. Here are key questions that individuals may want to ask before making decisions:

• Does the choice help me grow in my partnership with God?
• Does the choice turn me away from God?
• Am I claiming this choice as God's will simply to justify what I want—or what someone else wants me to do?
• Are my actions truly prompted by God—or by what others will say or think about me?[1]

In Romans 12:2 Paul wrote, "Do not be conformed to this world, but be transformed by the renewing of your minds, so that you may discern what is the will of God—what is good and acceptable and perfect."

Sometimes in our rush to make a decision, we simply decide to put something to a vote, "letting the chips fall where they may." Sometimes voting on an issue immediately sets up two poles, those for and those against. And often as a result there is either a battle or people simply walk away angry or hurt.

Discernment

Many Christians feel discernment is a better way to discover God's will than taking a vote. We can only know God's will by going directly to God. Danny Morris and Charles Olsen in *Discerning God's Will Together* (see Resources and References) outline a discernment process for use in a group setting. These suggestions are summarized below:

- *Framing*—What exactly are you trying to discern?
- *Grounding*—What value determines that this decision be made?
- *Shedding*—What preconceived notions, biases, and predetermined conclusions must I set aside to be truly open to God's will in this case?
- *Rooting*—What Christian tradition and/or biblical stories speak to this situation?
- *Listening*—What do others say/feel about the situation? Consider all options and needs.
- *Exploring*—Creatively explore all possibilities.
- *Improving*—Looking at each option and, with prayer, improve on it until it is the very best.
- *Weighing*—Sort out and test the options or paths in response to the leading of God's spirit.
- *Closing*—Close the explorations and identify the possible selection.
- *Resting*—Lay the choice before the heart of God and determine whether it brings a sense of peace and movement toward God or distress and movement away from God.

Traditions

Traditions are present in every church. Some traditions are long-standing and there may not even be an awareness of how they began. My husband and I were discussing the tradition of removing your hat when coming inside. This tradition, which many of us grew up with and respect, seems to be losing importance. The question is, what is its importance? How and where did this tradition begin and why? Is this tradition the same as removing one's shoes in the East? Is the original reason for such a tradition still legitimate? Questions like these are important to ask before deciding to continue a tradition.

Traditions are important to our stability and therefore precious to us. Often people feel threatened when someone attempts to alter their traditions. However, there are many occasions when a stronghold on a tradition may need to be released in order to accomplish a goal. At these times the importance of a tradition must be evaluated.

The responses to questions such as those listed below can help in the decision to hold on to a tradition, release it, or transform it.

- What is the origin of the tradition?
- What was the purpose of the tradition at its origin?
- Is that purpose still legitimate?
- How important is the tradition to my spiritual/emotional well-being?
- How important is the tradition to other persons' spiritual/emotional well-being? To whose?
- Does this tradition stand in the way of someone else's spiritual/emotional development?
- Can the tradition be altered with satisfaction for all concerned?
- Can a new tradition be established that will better accomplish the purpose and take the place of this one?
- Can this tradition and a new one coexist, accomplishing the purpose(s) intended?

Evaluations of traditions are important in any circumstances where we deal with other persons. Such evaluations help us to be more hospitable in our homes and also in our churches.[2]

There are also times when we must conform even if it is not what we prefer. An anthropology professor hated to wear earrings during an era when large earrings were popular. As a compromise, she chose to wear small ones after she discovered that people in professional circles seemed to respect her opinions more when she wore earrings. Conforming in minor things can result in people giving us more authority when it matters.

Spiritual Leadership

There was a time (and in many churches, still is) when we looked at the church as a "business." Our meetings were conducted strictly by Robert's Rules of Order, which often resulted in heated debates over issues. Church committee or board meetings were little different than that of a civic organization. Oh, yes, prayer was used to open a meeting and sometimes to close it as well, but those instances were only "book-end prayers" and seldom focused

on anything in particular. Disillusioned committee members often said, "When I accepted this job, I thought there would be a different environment in our meetings because it was the church. Instead I come away exhausted from battling over insignificant issues." My response was to explain that those in leadership in the church are only human, just like those outside the church.

I now have different expectations of church "business" meetings. If we cannot develop spiritual leadership within our committees and boards, then we are not following the calling of Christ. There is a better way, and only when we practice that better way will we become truly Christian. Everyone should come away from a church meeting challenged to carry out Christ's command, even when the meeting has been physically draining.

Charles Olsen, in *Transforming Church Boards into Communities of Spiritual Leaders* (see Resources and References), suggests that meetings be conducted as worshipful work. Olsen offers several formats for a meeting, such as patterning meetings like a worship service. This format, which I follow, is outlined below.

• We begin by offering praise to God, either in song or with a poem or scripture.

• Then move to sharing the story, expressions of ways that we have seen God at work in our lives or in the lives of others since we last met. These experiences can often be related to biblical stories.

• What would normally be called the agenda we label and look at as our offering.

This is what we are laying before God, seeking direction for the use of our gifts and talents.

• Throughout the time we encourage anyone who desires, to suggest that we pause for prayer for God's guidance. This prayer may be silent or vocal, but it undergirds all discussion and decisions.

• Then the "sending forth" is the plans that we make in order to carry out the decisions. And we leave, directing our plans and our lives to ministry.

What was surprising about this process was that, although meetings took a little longer the first few times we used it, we soon discovered that the meetings ran smoother and we were able to accomplish our mission in about the same amount of time. Yet we came away energized and excited about ministry. Our meetings were growing time for us spiritually.

Meeting Agendas and Follow-ups

Our fast-paced world and lives mean no one has time to come to the church just for the sake of attending a meeting. Therefore, time must be spent wisely. That is a part of the stewardship lifestyle that we as leaders must model and encourage. There are many ways of bringing folks together without actually calling a meeting. Consider conference calls or a mailing that asks people to respond by mail, e-mail, or phone, or by leaving messages on answering machines or voice mail. If your church has a Web page, why not set up a chat room for discussing various subjects.

No matter how you choose to "meet," make sure that the participants know what will be discussed ahead of time. Mail an agenda, or at least remind people of the topics to be discussed. Appendix 15 offers an excellent format that I find helpful. I create and distribute the agenda beforehand, and it helps everyone know what's before us and also provides an opportunity to take notes as we go along. In addition, the sample "Plan of Action" in appendix 16 can assist with any follow-up that is needed after the meeting.

Mission Statement Development

Whether you are working with a large church board or a small library committee, it is a good idea to develop a mission statement in order to have a clear understanding of your goals. Consider leading the group in an exercise of developing a mission statement using the following steps. It may be helpful for large committees to divide into three groups to accomplish the first three steps.

1. List on a large piece of paper the needs of individuals and families that your class and/or congregation should strive to meet. Post the list on the wall.
2. List on another large piece of paper the needs of the local community and world that your group and/or congregation should strive to meet. Post the list on the wall.
3. Study 1 Peter 2:1-10 and Acts 2:37-47 and list on another large piece of paper the qualities of a Christian congregation implicit in the passage. Post the list on the wall.
4. Looking at your lists on the wall, create a statement beginning with a phrase such as, "We are a people who . . ." or, "The mission of our committee is . . . ." Record your statement on a large paper.
5. When the rough draft is complete recite it in unison. Then pause for a moment of silent prayer and reflection, with everyone rereading the statement to themselves.

Work briefly on polishing any phrases, realizing that nothing is cast in stone. Be open to change and revision.

Working with Other Areas

As the church of the new millennium, we must climb out of our little territorial ministry cubicles and see the total mission of the church. We must share our dreams, our monies, and our volunteer resources. There are many ways that we can be helpful to other areas of the church in their ministry.

Worship and education can work together, not only in helping children to learn about worship (see "Children's Church" in chapter 1) but also in educating the congregation about worship. Consider placing a couple of sentences in the bulletin each week that will help everyone understand such things as the meaning of different colors for different seasons of the church year, why we stand for the first hymn (to recognize Christ as our king, as people stand when a king enters the room), and the meaning of various symbols that may be found in the sanctuary. If your responsibility includes the training of the

acolytes, a good resource is *Being an Acolyte* by Michael J. O'Donnell (See Resources and References).

Evangelism is the one area of the church that reaches out to new members. In the past, the practice was to wait until persons joined the church before involving them in leadership, and sometimes even in study. But the Baby Boomers and Generation Xers want to become involved in the church *before* they join. Develop studies that appeal to these generations. Plan a "Bible 101" course each year that offers a basic understanding of the Bible, and even helps students feel comfortable handling the Bible and finding specific passages. You will probably find older members who will attend the class as a "refresher" course. Encourage this. In addition, education can certainly help with confirmation (see chapter 5) and the classes for potential members. Plan these learning experiences in coordination with the evangelism committee, so that every event captures the teaching ministry of the entire church.

Stewardship is an area that often tries to function alone, because they see themselves as strictly the "money-raising" arm of the church. A reeducation needs to take place not only within the congregation, but also within the committee. (See "Stewardship" in chapter 6, page 52.)

Begin by including stewardship training for all ages during Sunday school. Contact a Christian bookstore or your denominational offices for resources on stewardship. Plan programs that help persons find their spiritual gifts, and then challenge them to use those gifts as good stewards. During a church-wide commitment emphasis, involve the children and youth by having them make posters expressing the things they like about the church or write litanies on ways we serve God through the church. In addition, help the stewardship committee create educational pieces on how the money raised is used, not only in the local congregation and neighborhood, but also in the denominational or world community.

Finally, missions is another area that often operates in its own sphere. As a means of raising the awareness of the congregation about faith in action, talk with mission leaders about the special mission emphasis your church supports, and develop educational displays about those missions. Many good mission studies are available; include a few of these as additional activities during weekly class sessions.

Celebration of Ministry

Although we are anxious to have persons volunteer to work with the programs in Christian education, we need to acknowledge that persons have the freedom to work in areas where they recognize God to be calling them. In fact, it may not always be in the church. Whether their ministry is in the church or in some other area of service to others, these persons should be recognized by the church. It would be good, at some point during the year, to recognize all those in the church who volunteer their services to help others in some way in both the church and the community. Here is a suggestion for planning such a celebration:

1. Through a questionnaire or interviews, find out what areas of the church and which ministries outside the church are serviced by members of your church.
2. Get a brief description of each of these ministries.
3. Create a collage of photographs of persons in your church serving in the various ministries.
4. Set a date to celebrate all those in your church who are in ministry in all these areas. Announce the celebration to the congregation.
5. Using the descriptions of the ministries, create a litany similar to the one at right:
   (Note: Each person responds with any and all groups that are appropriate to his or her ministry.)
6. On the day of the celebration provide a special ribbon for all those who are in ministry in some way.
7. In the bulletin, list all of the ministries represented in your congregation. If your church is small enough that you know that you have listed the ministry of all those in the church, list their names beside the ministry. If you are uncertain you may decide not to list names.
8. Use celebrative hymns along with the litany during the service.
9. Follow the service with a gathering and refreshments.

Pastor:	Christ set the example of caring for others. We follow that example as a caring church. Some of us fulfill God's calling within the church, and some fulfill that calling in other agencies in the community.
Group 1:	Some of us care for children.
Group 2:	Some of us work with youth.
Group 3:	Some of us work with all ages of adults.
Pastor:	All of these for whom we care are God's children.
Group 4:	Some of us help to give Christ's healing touch to others.
Group 5:	Some of us use hammers and saws and other tools in our ministry for others.
Group 6:	Some of us prepare or deliver food in our ministry.
Group 7:	Some of us use automobiles, computers, telephones, and other equipment in our ministry.
All:	We all put our hearts into our ministry.
Pastor:	We celebrate these ministries and the many persons in our church who carry them out.
All:	Caring for others is a way of extending Christ's hands through the centuries and around the world. Thank you, God, for calling us to ministry. Amen.

1. Halverson, Delia, *Living Simply* (Nashville: Abingdon Press, 1996), p. 20.
2. Halverson, Delia, *The Gift of Hospitality* (St. Louis: Chalice Press, 1999), pp. 77-78.

Routines, Rituals, and Rally Days

There are many occasions in a family's life when they are particularly interested in participating in the church. Although we no longer celebrate the passages of life as we did hundreds of years ago, perhaps we should reexamine their importance. Listed below are special transitions in people's lives where the church can offer support. Also, included are suggestions of ways of celebrating the occasion, as well as ideas for studies or other support opportunities.

Weddings

• Announce these events in newsletter and bulletins.

• Sponsor a seminar for youth on the commitment of marriage.

• Affirm long-time commitment in marriage by celebrating anniversaries. (see "Birthdays and Wedding Anniversaries")

Prenatal

• Encourage prospective parents to volunteer in the infant nursery before their child is born in order to familiarize themselves with the nursery.

• Offer classes or support groups on the birthing process. Consider sponsoring the event and asking an outside organization to do the teaching. By inviting attendance from the community, potential members are introduced to the church.

• Present soon-to-be parents with a gift book. Generally, prior to the birth is a more appropriate time for this type of gift since there is more time to read.

Birth/adoption of a child

• Provide classes or support groups for parents.

• Place a rose on the altar, which is then given to the parents.

• Give parents a gift book that will help them begin sharing their faith with the child. *How Do Our Children Grow?* offers suggestions for everyday sharing of faith.

• Place a needlework quilt or wall hanging in the church with name and birth date of the child.

• Send a letter to the parents congratulating them and telling them of the programs you have to offer for the new child and also for themselves as parents.

• Present a letter and bookmark to older sibling(s) rejoicing in the birth of their sibling.

Birthdays and wedding anniversaries

• Encourage teachers to send postcards to students on their birthdays and wedding anniversaries.

• Celebrate everyone's birthday and wedding anniversary that occurs that week during a midweek dinner. Remember to set aside an evening when you celebrate the birthdays that fall during the months that you don't have midweek dinners.

• List birthdays and wedding anniversaries in the newsletter.

• Celebrate long-time marriages during worship by recognizing everyone who has been married over a given length of time. Find out how many years each couple has been married, add these together, and celebrate the total number of years. (Some churches shy away from recognizing anniversaries for fear of embarrassing people who are divorced. However, celebrating anniversaries affirms the lasting commitments these individuals have made to one another.)

Stay-at-home parent

• Offer Mom/Dad-and-Me playtime once a week for very young children.

• Provide a parents' program during the day (see appendix 17).

• Sponsor a Parent's Morning Out program or babysitting coop.
Beginning preschool, Sunday school, public school

• Send a congratulatory letter to the child.

• Recognize these children in a worship service.

• Present each student with a pencil, ruler, or fabric lunch bag with the church's name on it, perhaps saying "You're special to God and to us at _____ Church."

Receiving Bibles

• List names of those receiving Bibles in the bulletin and newsletter. Most churches give Bibles at the beginning of the third or fourth grade. Remember to give a Bible that is appropriate to the age.

• Plan a half-day study for Bible recipients and their parents where they explore some of the fundamentals of the Bible together. This begins the parent/child opportunities of reading the Bible together and is a nonthreatening way for adults who are unfamiliar with the Bible to learn along with their child.

• Send follow-up letters to Bible recipients six months later, reminding them of some special helps in the Bible. These helps might be included on a bookmark that is enclosed in the letter.

• Give students a subscription to a children's devotional magazine such as *Pockets*, which includes Bible study.

Confirmation

• Sponsor weekly classes for students and a separate class for their parents where they study the same materials and where ways to discuss the study at home during the week are suggested. The classes could meet during Sunday school, with the parent class acting as a support group for parents of young teens.

• Develop a mentoring program for students with adults other than their parents. Recognize and dedicate the mentors in a worship service. After the program, write a letter of appreciation to mentors. In the fall of the next year, again write to the mentors asking that they contact their students, affirm them, and encourage them to live out their faith during the new school year. Consider expanding this program so that the mentors follow the teen through the high school years.

• Recognize those who were confirmed the year before during the confirmation service, perhaps involving them in leadership of the service, or asking that they read a special statement during a litany.

Entering middle school or junior high

• Provide an orientation course on "Life in Middle School," covering the questions they have about middle school and also reminding them that the church is still a part of their life even when they are away from the church building. Ask a middle-school teacher or administrator to be a part of this class. Ask rising ninth graders to assist with the course and make up a little booklet of suggestions of how to keep their faith in middle school.

• Arrange to visit students at schools and have lunch with them in the cafeteria.

• Designate a special Sunday when representatives from the high school class visit the rising middle school/junior high students' class and invite them to come to their new class. When they arrive, have the rest of the class create a celebrative atmosphere.

Graduates from elementary, high school, college, vocational training, and so forth

• Recognize students in a worship service.

• List names in the bulletin and newsletter.

• Give each person a gift (example, devotional or journal) that they can use in their next stage of life.

• Start an "Adopt a College Student" program where each student is "adopted" by someone in the church and is sent notes, postcards, birthday cards, occasional care packages, and so forth.

• Sponsor a college students' reunion during a

holiday. This can be as simple as juice and bagels during Sunday school hour, or as complex as a cookout on Sunday night. Allow ample time for renewing friendships.

• Use a special invitation to those who are graduating, inviting them to attend a special meeting with the "age group" they are moving up to.

Career change

• Send a letter of recognition and acknowledging prayers during this exciting but apprehensive time.

• Write or call the person on the anniversary of a career change.

Job loss or unemployment

• Provide a support group for those seeking jobs.

• Start a job list or bulletin board where members

can post job opportunities they are aware of.

• Send a letter or offer verbal assurance that the situation is being prayed for by a prayer chain.

• Celebrate with the person (verbally or by letter) when he or she finds employment.

Commissioning to short-term mission work

• Provide some form of financial support from the church for every short-term mission experience, whether individual or group. This gesture affirms the church's support of each member becoming involved in hands-on mission.

• Hold a special commissioning service before mission participants leave for their project. (Review your church hymnal or worship book for suggestions.)

• Send letters or cards encouraging individuals or groups whose projects are a week's length or more. If available, contact them frequently through e-mail.

• Celebrate the work that was accomplished when they return. Provide an opportunity for sharing their experiences with the entire church.

• Present a certificate of appreciation for the service rendered.

Keep up the good work.

• Prepare a picture display of the mission experience. If available, add the pictures to the church web page.

Commitment to church-related vocation

• Send letter of affirmation to individuals after their decision has been made.

• Offer a special recognition of this decision during worship. (Review your church hymnal or worship resource for liturgical suggestions.)

• Maintain contact with the person if their work moves them to a new location.

• Celebrate (or at least name) everyone who has moved into church-related vocations from your church.

Cancer survival anniversary

• Send a letter celebrating the anniversary and encouraging the individual.

• Offer a support group for cancer survivors.

• Ask prayer groups within the church to offer prayers of celebration and support.

Divorce

• Sponsor divorce recovery workshops.

• Provide support group.

• Offer counseling referral or on-site counselor.

Second marriage/stepfamilies

• Provide a course such as "Considering Marrying Again."

• Offer stepfamily support group.

• Sponsor a course for children on dealing with stepparents and new siblings.

First apartment

• Send a congratulatory letter or card.

• Plan a shower of essentials or food stuffs, sponsored by a Sunday school class or other small group.

Giving up driver's license

• Celebrate the ministry that the person has carried on throughout his or her driving career. This may occur for an individual within a small group, or within the entire church for all those who gave up their license during the year.

• Send a letter recognizing an individual's past ministry using their car.

Disabilities/Handicapping situations

• Offer support groups.

• Provide accessibility to the church facility.

• Provide hearing enhancement/signing/large print Bibles and hymnals.

Illnesses

• Send letters and cards.

• Post messages/banners from Sunday school class.

• Provide meals for the family.

Learning disabilities
- Offer support groups for both students and parents.
- Sponsor workshop/information for teachers on ways to deal with various learning disabilities.

Members moving from town
- Highlight and celebrate the past fellowship that was shared.
- Contact a church in their new community.
- Send follow-up letters to ensure that the previous member has located a new church family.

Military service sign-up
- Send letters of support.
- Give a travel-size Bible.
- Hold a reunion with peers when individual returns to town.

Natural disasters
- Establish a disaster plan ahead of time.
- Offer prayer support.
- Assist in recovery.
- Sponsor a seminar on understanding God's role in disaster.

New home or apartment
- Offer a service of dedication/blessing for the home.
- Give a Christian symbol for the front door or other appropriate gift.
- Send a letter of celebration.

Receiving driver's license
- Offer a study on stewardship of the use of car.
- Celebrate the dedication of the driver's license.

Retirement
- Celebrate the service the member has given.

- Offer a seminar on preparation for retirement.
- Suggest new ways to be in ministry.
- Provide information on economical travel that is meaningful and educational.

Returning adult children
- Send a welcome letter with an invitation to appropriate events and programs.
- Offer support group for parents.

Death of a family member
- Provide support groups for children and youth as well as for adults.
- Sponsor seminar on understanding death.
- Suggest a grief mentor.
- Schedule a seminar on living wills, death with dignity, organ donor, and so forth.

Special achievement (honor award, sports, publish book, or other achievement)
- Send a letter of recognition.
- Recognize person in newsletter.

Assisted living move
- Offer seminars on choosing a facility.
- Celebrate the role that the person's private home has had in their life and ministry to others.
- Take a quality photograph of the home and frame it for the person to take with him or her.
- Start an estate sale service. (One church began this ministry when a member's family could not hold the sale. They discovered not only a way to minister to the family, but also a means of raising money for missions. Sometimes the sales are held in the home and other times at the church. An additional service would be to clean the home and prepare it for sale.)

Special Sundays

During a Christmas Eve service I looked around the congregation and noticed many persons who did not attend regularly.

Then I looked at the information in our bulletin and tried to put myself in the place of these people. I realized that if this was their only contact with our church, they had no way of knowing that we have a regular fellowship dinner every Wednesday, support groups, or a softball team every spring.

There are many traditional holidays or special occasions when families are more likely to attend church than others, such as Christmas, Easter, Mother's/Father's Day, baptisms and confirmation. Often special occasions are highlighted during these times, but not opportunities for outreach. When a family rarely comes to church, we need to provide information about programs and events that might be of interest. Consider preparing a bulletin insert with brief descriptions of various programs and studies.

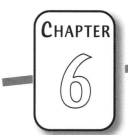
Seasons, Sacraments, and Stewardship

Expectations help to ground our faith to life. There is a rhythm in the seasons of nature, in the way our families grow up and mature, and even in the events in the church. As educators and leaders we do well to work with these patterns that give us stability and balance.

Seasons

The seasons of the Christian year create a rhythm that helps us remember the life of Christ. Instead of looking at the seasons as repetitive events that occur year after year, we must begin seeing the year as a flow through our contemporary lives, a living out of the faith story each year. Built into these seasons are special things that we do and see and hear, even things that we smell and touch that awaken our senses to seeing Christ anew all around us.

A good resource for understanding the church year is *The Special Days and Seasons of the Christian Year.*

The following are suggestions for ways to help people understand and appreciate the seasons.

• Make and display banners.

• On the Sunday that the colors change, have a family bring the paraments (altar cloths and visuals) forward and drape them in the presence of the worshipers. Include placing the stole over the pastor's shoulders.

• Place explanatory statements in the bulletin.

• Use appropriate colors and symbols in classrooms.

• On the first Sunday of each season, suggest that people wear clothing of the appropriate color.

• Create a booklet explaining seasons, symbols, stained glass windows, banners, and so forth. Distribute copies to the congregation and keep a supply on hand for visitors and guests.

Sacraments

Sacrament means *sacred moment.* It is a time when we feel that we come in contact with the divine. We use symbolic elements to help us taste, touch, feel, know, and experience God's grace (love) in Christ. Although

Catholics observe seven sacraments, most Protestant churches celebrate only the two that Jesus participated in, baptism and Communion (i.e., Eucharist, Last Supper, or Lord's Supper).

• *Baptism* indicates the grace (love) of God at work in each person's life through the church. There are three forms of baptism: *sprinkling, pouring,* and *immersion.*

• *Communion* has its roots in the Jewish celebration of the Passover. It is a time when we remember Jesus and realize that God is a part of each one of us.

Listed below are ideas for making the sacraments more meaningful. See *How Do Our Children Grow?* chapter 8, for age-appropriate suggestions on baptism and Communion, as well as more details regarding the following suggestions.

• As you begin the baptism service, pour the water from a pitcher from a height of a couple of feet. This allows the sound to penetrate the sanctuary and even mists those nearby, alerting our senses.

• Invite children to come to the front of the sanctuary prior to a baptism and explain a little about it. Let them feel the water.

• Conduct classes for parents before infant baptism.

• Use a shell to lift and pour the water at baptism, and then give the shell to the person or parents of the child being baptized.

• After a young child's baptism, lead or carry the child into the congregation to meet his or her church family.

• Write a letter to the person being baptized or the parents of a child being baptized, expressing your

Season	Time	Color	Symbols
Advent (*from the Latin word for "coming," adventus*)	Four Sundays before and up to Christmas	purple (*royalty*) or blue (*Mary's color—hope*)	wreath (*God's eternal love*) evergreens (*ever-living*) candle (*Christ as light of world*) trumpets (*prophecy*) Jesse tree (*symbols of Jesus' ancestors—see Isaiah 11:1*)
Christmas	Christmas Eve and 12 days after, to Epiphany	white (*coming of light*)	Chrismon tree nativity scene angels Christmas star Poinsettia, rose
Epiphany	January 6	white and gold	three crowns (*Note: number of kings is not biblical but tradition*) three gifts Christmas star
Season After Epiphany	Days between Jan. 6 and Ash Wed.	1st and last Sundays—white; others—green	baptismal font, shell (*Jesus' baptism*) water jars (*miracle at Cana*) green plant (*life/ministry of Christ*)
Lent	Ash Wednesday to Easter	purple (*royalty, penitence*)	rough cross veil over cross remove shiny objects and flowers
Holy Week	week before Easter Palm Sunday Maundy Thursday Good Friday	purple or red black (*darkness*)	coins, whip, crown of thorns, and so forth palm branches grapes, bread, chalice, foot washing cross draped black—no altar cloths
Easter	Easter Sunday to Pentecost	white, gold and festive colors	flowers (*particularly those grown from dried "dead" bulbs*) empty cross/tomb butterfly and cocoon peacock (*sheds and regrows feathers*) phoenix (*mythical bird rose from ashes*)
Pentecost	50th day after Easter	red (*fire or the Holy Spirit*)	flame of fire doves red flowers ship (*ship*) rainbow
Season after Pentecost	Day after Pentecost to Advent	green (*growth in Christ*)	triangle (*on Trinity Sunday*) green plant

[Some churches choose to extend the Pentecost Season, celebrating outreach to people of all nations as they remember the gift of languages at Pentecost. See Acts 2.]

joy and offering assistance in helping the adult or child continue to grow in faith.

• Conduct a parent/child workshop on either or both sacraments. (See appendix 25.)

• Invite a family to go with the pastor to serve Communion to a homebound person.

• Ask different families to bake the bread that is used in Communion and process with the loaf down the aisle at the beginning of the service.

• Invite classes to take turns preparing the Communion elements.

• Have classes make a cloth to cover the bread.

• Ask different families to bring a white linen cloth from home to use as the cover for the bread.

Stewardship

A section on stewardship in a book on Christian education may seem a bit out of place, however it is included for two reasons. First, it is important that the relationship between stewardship and Christian education be recognized (see "Working with Other Areas" on page 44). As leaders, we must work together in every aspect of the church. Second, when we teach stewardship, then we strengthen our educational program with devoted volunteers who recognize their talents as gifts to be used for God.

The early church illustrated a lifestyle of giving. They gave of themselves and their money to carry the message to others, while caring for those in need. Later, when the church and state united, priests and staff were hired, thus moving the opportunity for lay involvement away from the people. During this time, budget needs were paid by the government and financed through taxes. There was no need to raise money to repair the roof! In addition, the outreach mission of the church was financed through taxes, so the true meaning of giving was lost. Tithing for the early Christians was a governmental controlled part of each person's tax responsibility.

Much later, in countries such as the United States where church and state are separate, the need to raise funds reasserted itself. It became commonplace to use volunteers to carry out the mission and work of the church. In the panic to pay bills, church leaders began putting the "cart before the horse," and for years raised funds for ministry and mission without educating their congregations about the true meaning of stewardship. Thus, stewardship became simply a matter of finance.

Our challenge now is to educate people about something that should have been a part of their Christian experience all along. When our congregations understand that all that we have is a gift from God, and when we learn how to recognize and really appreciate our individual gifts, then tithing of our time, talents, and money becomes our act of thanks to God.

The teaching of this lesson falls logically on the shoulders of the education unit of the church, however as long as we continue to operate as a separate ministry area, we will be unable to master the task before us. One of the best ways to teach stewardship is to practice stewardship in the Christian education program and to call attention to the fact that the church does practice good stewardship. Outlined below are suggestions for promoting church stewardship.

• Hold seminars and preach sermons on recognizing our gifts.

• Respect and support those who use their gifts in service through the church and through other caring organizations such as hospitals, Habitat for Humanity, and so forth.

• Recycle materials from classrooms and offices.

• Practice good stewardship of people's time by honoring beginning and ending times for meetings.

• Help families practice stewardship of their time and gasoline by clustering meetings, and even setting one night aside for family time.

• Encourage conservation of fuel by carpooling or using a church van.

• Find persons or other congregations that need items you plan to discard and give the items away.

• Take pride in the facility, making repairs promptly, keeping carpets clean, and so forth.

• Keep equipment in good working order.

• Use only biodegradable and nontoxic supplies.

• Use china plates and stainless flatware instead of Styrofoam, paper, or plastic. Although washing them after use takes a little more time, in the long run this practice is better for the environment.

• Do not use food for craft activities unless you plan to eat it afterward.

• Give flowers from the altar to the members who are ill or hospitalized.

• Practice water conservation.

• Turn lights off when not in use.

• Conserve fuel by heating and cooling only necessary spaces.

One of the best books for adults on stewardship is *Don't Shoot the Horse ('til You Know How to Drive the Tractor)* by Herb Mather.

Teachers (and Other Volunteers), Training, and Tending

Jesus is the prime example of a good teacher. Frequently we refer to stories that Jesus told in his teaching, but he used other methods effectively too. Typically he took an everyday item or an everyday experience and used it as an illustration. Jesus taught with questions that challenged his listeners to think beyond their usual boundaries. He listened to others and knew his students, adapting his teaching methods to the people to whom he was speaking. A student of the scriptures himself, Jesus used them in his teaching, encouraging commitment from others while exhibiting commitment himself, even to his death. Every portion of Jesus' life exhibited a close relationship with God, and this relationship gave Jesus authority. What better way to learn to teach than to look to the scriptures? The scriptures also tell us to teach in order to pass on the faith (Deuteronomy 4:9-10; 6:1-9; 31:12). Jesus commanded us: "Go to the people of all nations and make them my disciples. Baptize them in the name of the Father, the Son, and the Holy Spirit, and teach them to do everything I have told you. I will be with you always, even until the end of the world" (Matthew 28:19-20 CEV).

Teaching is a true calling, rather than simply an obligation. The teaching ministry in your church will be much more effective if it is referred to as a ministry and as a call to teach, instead of focusing so heavily on recruitment. Work with your education committee to develop a *terms of call* for teachers. Include a covenant where the church covenants with the teacher, and the teacher covenants with the church. Consider this example:

Terms of Call

Jesus called his disciples as he began his ministry. At the close of his ministry on earth, he commissioned them, and all who followed them, to "Go, then, to all peoples everywhere and make them my disciples" (Matthew 28:19a TEV).

As you respond to Christ's call to teach, _____ Church covenants with each teacher that:

The church will:	The teacher will:
• pray and support teachers as a congregation	• spend time preparing
• provide curriculum materials	• be in the classroom before the session
• provide training experiences	• attend worship and be a part of total church
• provide leadership and resource persons	• know persons in his/her class and recognize their needs
• provide supplies, audio-visuals, etc.	• attend and participate in planning
• provide clean, furnished rooms	• show and share his/her faith
• provide support and help from pastor and staff	• use curriculum approved by church
• provide opportunities for personal Christian growth	• attend training events whenever possible[1]

Job (Mission) Descriptions

How can they know unless we tell them? A part of our problem with finding good volunteers results from the era when most people grew up in the church and knew what each job entailed. Everyone knew that the education committee made their plans in October for the Christmas party in December. In fact, it was expected to be on a special Sunday in December, and no one even had to put it on a calendar. Likewise, the date for vacation Bible school was always the same, and the same mothers always volunteered. This was an opportunity for those mothers to spend some creative time outside the home, and they came away feeling rewarded with a boosted self-esteem.

But life in the church isn't that way anymore! Most parents in our churches work outside of the home, and those who don't are trying to carry the load of all the volunteer positions that were necessary in the past. Our well of anxious volunteers has gone dry. In addition, many of the young adults who are coming into our churches do not already know their volunteer responsibilities. We can't ask them to lead a committee or to teach a class and then ignore them. They need training and guidance. And their time restraints will determine whether and how well they do the job. They need to know what they are getting into before they sign up. Therefore, it is more important than ever to develop mission (job) descriptions. Appendixes 18 and 19 include a sample mission description for a Children's Coordinator, and a teaching job description. Your unique church situation will dictate the changes that may need to be made to the material.

Finding Volunteers

It is essential to recruit teachers who are caring persons, have good communication skills, have a basic knowledge of the Bible, and set an example of Christian standards and faithfulness to the church. Moreover, volunteers who support your educational endeavors in other ways will need to be recruited. In addition to the basic skills required to carry out their jobs, these persons will also need to be caring and committed to Christ and the church.

Although there are many ways to search for volunteers, many churches rely on a printed announcement in the newsletter or bulletin. The following is a list of alternative places and ways to search for new teachers and volunteers. For more detailed information regarding this area see *How to Train Volunteer Teachers* (see Resources and References).

- *Be in continual prayer for God's guidance.*
- *Know the congregation.*
- *Know persons individually.* Attend all the meetings and class parties you can manage. Talk both collectively and individually with adult class members and ask for suggestions. Search out new members and speak to visitors.
- *Develop your own personnel information file* (see "Awareness" in chapter 1, page 9).
- *Use talent cards and interest surveys.* Many churches maintain this information by computer. As you review the list, add your own notes and look for "hints of leadership."
- *Make calls to members or regular attendees who have not become involved.* Ask, "How can we help you to be in ministry?" Look for ways to involve people, instead of looking for folks to be involved.
- *Ask persons who said no previously because of a lack of time.* Their circumstances may have changed.

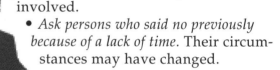

Consider Theological Perspective

It is important that your teachers' theological viewpoints do not clash with those of your church. Hopefully, independent thinking is encouraged in your church, however, it is best to avoid someone in the classroom who has a completely opposing view or who cannot tolerate diversity of belief.

Teachers of children are primarily advocates of the faith, telling and pointing the way. As children grow and move into their teen years and even as adults, they need *clarifiers* of the faith, teachers and mentors who can help them clarify their own beliefs. These teachers encourage students to inquire and question, to ask themselves, "Is this what I really believe, or am I just accepting it because someone else told me this?"

The Hebrew word, *emunah*, can be translated into faith. I like to define *faith* as a total trust and confidence in God. It involves our relationship with God and how that relationship grows and develops. Faith links us with God and with others. Belief, on the other hand, is what we believe at one time or another. The meaning of our beliefs may change. Belief is independently owned and cannot be forced on another person. In *Will Our Children Have Faith?* John Westerhoff III (see Resources and References) outlines our faith growth in four styles:

- **Experienced Faith:** observing and copying, acting and reacting to surroundings and people, exploring and testing

- **Affiliated Faith:** belonging (relationships, groups), expressing feelings, authority (this is OUR story)

- **Searching Faith:** opportunity to question, commitment to cause with actions, critical judgment, experimentation

- **Owned Faith:** personal belief, identity (open to other's view/sure of own), witness to others, integrity (belief in action)

Children function out of the experienced and affiliated styles of faith. Mid to older teens and certainly young adults move into the searching style. However, if clarifiers are not provided or if people are ridiculed for questioning, then they will reject everything and turn away. Although some adults will never feel comfortable in the searching style of faith, we should encourage inquiring and questioning as part of all adult classrooms. Our faith is stagnant if we do not continue to question until we die.

Learning about the styles of faith is important to every teacher, regardless of the age that they teach. *How to Train Volunteer Teachers* includes a mini-retreat that can help in this area.

Appendix 21 offers questions for teachers that may be useful when thinking about their theological perspective. These questions will not automatically label the teachers, but will offer guidance in how they will likely approach the students in the classroom. Consider using the questions in a couple of ways:

- *Use them as a questionnaire in a workshop atmosphere.* Afterward, ask the participants to discuss their answer to each question with a partner and then share any observations with the entire group. Collect the questionnaires. Tell everyone to expect to receive their questionnaire by mail at the close of the year so that they can see how their ideas have changed through a year of teaching. This provides an excellent opportunity to review their statements and gain a better understanding of their theological perspectives.

- *Use individual questions as you talk with teachers on a one-to-one basis.* This should be an informal conversation, not "read from script" interview.

Short and Long-term Teaching

Teachers are often hesitant to commit to a long term of teaching, so it is wise to covenant with your teachers for only one year at a time. This not only works well for your teachers but it offers an opportunity to adjust your teaching staff at the end of each year.

Make it a practice to have your teaching list approved by the education committee. Then, if a change needs to be made, present the proposal to the education committee for their support. This support will be important, particularly if the need arises to ask a teacher to step out of the classroom and into another ministry.

Everyone who has worked in Christian education for any length of time has at least one story to tell of a miss match of a teacher with a class. This may happen because the teacher is working with the wrong age group, or perhaps took the job out of duty or even with a lot of zeal, but teaching is not his or her gift. In such cases, locate other places that the person can serve within the church. Sometimes, taking a positive approach helps in convincing the person to switch.

Although several possibilities for shorter-term teaching exist, avoid having two teachers rotating a teaching assignment from week to week, where one teacher is on one week and off the next. This does not allow consistency in teaching. Even one month on and one month off does not provide adequate time for proper relationships to develop. You will have some students who only come one or possibly two weeks out of the month, and for them the teacher shifts each time they attend. A commitment to teaching should be at least a quarterly (three-month) term.

Cycle Teaching

If your teachers cannot commit for nine months or the full year, consider cycle teaching as a means of sharing the responsibility. This format allows teachers to move back into their adult class for six months out of the year. Although the cycle model requires more teachers in the long run, teachers benefit from the break from teaching and more consistent contact with their own classes.

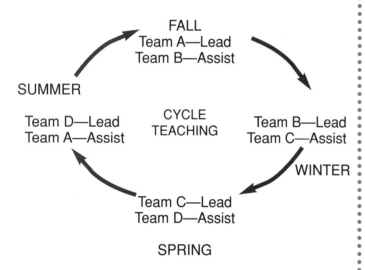

In-Cycle Teaching:
• No one must be away from their adult class for more than two quarters at a time.
• There is continuity from quarter to quarter.
• One team may take a Sunday off without losing continuity because the other team has been in the classroom and can step in.
• If both teams need to take off, there is a backup team that has taught that particular class before.

• Better adult/child relationships are created. The adult classes from which the teams come have an interest in the children's class. They might invite the children to share something they are doing (songs, drama, and so forth) or hold a party for them.
• The teams are more likely to sign up year after year with no "burnout."

Adult Class Liaison

One way to help teachers feel connected to an adult class is by asking each class to appoint a liaison to keep those working outside the classroom on Sundays informed of what's happening in the class. The liaison would pass on information about celebrations and concerns of class members and keep teachers apprised of social events. Tapes could also be made of special class sessions and passed on through the liaison.

Ministry Fair

In order to help persons explore ways that they can serve God through the church, we need to educate them about service opportunities. One of the easiest ways to do this is through a ministry fair. This allows an opportunity for all areas of the church to display the workings of their ministries. Often, fairs are held on a Sunday morning so that people can view the displays before and after worship and Sunday school. Each committee, study group, or other ministry sets up a table and provides a representative available to answer questions as people move about the fair. Balloons and other decorations make the occasion festive and inviting. Consider including these items on the tables:
• Pictures or video of events carried out by committee
• Pictures or video of a committee or group at work or studying
• Samples of a study group's curriculum or study materials
• Printed statements from committee members of what they enjoy about working with that committee
• A brochure describing the committee with a list of opportunities for serving through the committee
• A sign-up sheet for events or for service opportunities through the committee
• Display of items used by that area (such as paraments for worship committee, scissors and crayons for children's committee, recording of Christian rock music for youth committee, hammers and saws for a mission project)

Affirming Volunteers

Most churches try to thank their teachers in some way. They may have a potluck dinner for them or present them with a gift in the spring. Even though these special celebrations are appreciated, it is important to affirm volunteers throughout the year. If the affirmations are visible to the entire church, then others also become interested in being a part of the educational ministry.

Maintaining contact with your volunteers lets them know that you appreciate what they are doing. For example, I sometimes send a postcard to my teachers when I am on vacation. It's something that I can do easily while riding or during a relax time. Sometimes I even print out labels that I take along so that I don't have to address the cards.

Teacher NEWSLETTER and Handbooks

Teachers need to know what's going on in your educational program and to have resources available. A bimonthly or monthly newsletter will help them feel up-to-date. The newsletter can be as simple as a copy of a magazine article with a note attached to a formal newsletter with articles that pertain specifically to your church. If you do use magazine articles, contact the publisher for permission before copying and distributing copies to teachers. Appendix 23 provides a form for helping you plan and organize newsletters.

No matter how familiar your teachers are with your educational program, it is a good idea to develop a handbook, or at least a few pages of information for the teachers. See appendix 24 for more detailed information on planning a teacher handbook.

Curriculum Fair

Plan a curriculum fair to acquaint teachers with the resources that your church has to offer. Display all of the curriculum resources (for example, printed materials, videotapes, audiotapes) that are for teaching use. Plan this event for a Sunday morning, and encourage all adults to visit the display sometime during the morning. Most will be surprised at what is available.

Training Opportunities

You must plan your training opportunities according to the needs and schedules of your teachers. In addition, when deciding what type of training to offer, recognize that teachers learn in different ways, just as students learn differently.

It is important to do whatever possible to make it easy for teachers to attend the training. First and foremost, child care is a must. I suggest stating in the publicity that child care will be available by reservation. Then if you know of a teacher that may need this service, consider calling to ask if she or he will need it.

• *The time of training events is of prime importance.* Work with your teachers to set the best time. This may take a series of trial and error, and may change as your staff changes.

Weeknight training works well for some churches. Canvas your teachers before deciding on the day *and* the time. Pairing the training with a meal may help their schedule with family responsibilities; in that case, a meal for the entire family should be considered.

Saturday morning may be a good time. Most people will prefer to gather as early as 8:30 A.M. and be finished by midmorning or at least before noon. This gives them the rest of the day to plan family events or run errands.

Sunday morning is another option. Several years ago I would never have suggested teacher training on Sunday mornings. However, the schedules of many teachers leaves Sunday morning as the only time available. If you do hold a training event on Sunday, leave the worship hour open and plan to sit together in worship. Sometimes churches ask parents or former teachers to teach a class so that teachers can have an extended time of training.

Sunday lunch works for some teachers. Here again, if a meal is planned, include the whole family, or at least invite teachers to bring sack lunches for their children. Provide child care during the training.

Sunday evening while the youth group meets may be a good time for your Sunday morning teachers if they have youth. However, if you plan to include the youth group leaders, you will need to choose another time.

• **Types of training**

Regular interval training offers stability for teachers. Participants can put the date on their calendar and plan around it. Depending on your teaching staff, it can be monthly, bimonthly, or quarterly. Most churches find quarterly training fits best into their schedule, along with an occasional special event training. Quarterly meetings are also a good time to distribute and discuss new curriculum.

A teacher training course for several weeks is good preparation for persons who haven't taught before or who are exploring the idea of teaching. Include actual time in the classroom for observing good teachers.

Apprenticeship is one of the easiest ways to train

individual teachers if you have a Master Teacher. A new teacher serves as an assistant in the classroom; and after a few weeks of observing, is given more and more responsibility, under the guidance of the Master Teacher.

Master Teachers' classrooms can serve as observation classrooms. For example, a teacher who is struggling with discipline could observe a Master Teacher's classroom. Afterward, perhaps over lunch, the teacher could ask the Master Teacher such questions as, "Why did you do this?" or "How did you know the child needed that?"

One-on-one training may be necessary on occasion, particularly if you have a teacher coming in during the middle of the year who is hesitant about teaching. This might be accompanied by some type of self-directed study.

Self-directed study should be encouraged for all teachers, even if they have taught for some years. *32 Ways to Become a Great Sunday School Teacher* (see Resources and References) offers a variety of topics for self-directed study. When teachers work with a self-directed study, plan a debriefing time for those using the study to meet together for discussion.

Plan at least one special event training each year. Focus on various topics, such as teaching prayer, using puppets, or even a time of personal enrichment for the teachers. Or invite a guest to lead the training. Prior to the event, share with that person some of the things you particularly want to get across to the teachers. I've led workshops in churches and related the same information that the staff person has said for years. But because it came from someone outside their church, the teachers were more receptive.

Attending district or regional events should be encouraged for your teachers. Consider offering financial support for teachers who attend these events. If nothing else, teachers will benefit from exposure to the teachers from other churches. Another benefit is that these events sometimes bring in experts who motivate the teachers.

As you develop your training plan, review appendix 22. Include these categories in your planning:

1. Orientation and interpretation
   (information, goals, curriculum)

2. Support
   (group building, get acquainted, and so forth)

3. Spiritual growth
   (Bible study, prayer, stewardship, spiritual formation)

4. Teaching method
   (storytelling, puppets, music, and so forth)

Support with Prayer

Even though I encountered some of the best Christian education professors in my academic training, I do not recall anyone suggesting that we deliberately include Prayer Partners in our recruitment of volunteers. The need for this became evident one year when I was out of town during vacation Bible school. Sensing that the teachers needed additional support, we recruited a Prayer Partner for each class. It was so successful that we did the same thing for every class in the fall. Here are pointers that will help you develop Prayer Partners for your classes.

• Invite persons to act as Prayer Partners for individual classes through announcements and personal contact.

• Involve persons who otherwise have no leadership in this area in order to help more persons in the church know what is happening in education. This also gives persons who are homebound an outlet for ministry.

• Ask Prayer Partners to pray regularly for the teachers and class members, particularly on Sundays.

• Furnish the Prayer Partner with:
 —written information on prayer at an introductory meeting .
 —names, addresses, and phone numbers of teachers and students in the class. (A picture of the class would also be nice, with the names identified.)
 —information on the subjects the class will study each quarter.

• Give the teachers and classes the name, address, and phone number of the Prayer Partner.

• Encourage the teachers to contact the Prayer Partner regularly as well as at times when they have a special need for prayer, such as a particularly hard subject or when there are discipline problems with a particular student.

• Ask the class to write and thank the person for acting as their Prayer Partner.

• Invite Prayer Partners to visit their classes early in the year so that the students can recognize him or her when they meet in the building.

• Periodically throughout the year drop a card to the Prayer Partners, asking them to contact the teachers about something specific, such as sending a note of thanks for their teaching ministry at Thanksgiving or a valentine note in February.

• List the Prayer Partners in the bulletin alongside the teachers on Education Sunday.

• Recognize Prayer Partners, including an appreciation event at the end of the year, whenever teachers are recognized.

Prayer is as important in the workings of the church as any other ministry. If we do not surround our planning and our actions with prayer, we miss a strong support.

Pray for Your Volunteers

Your prayer for volunteers and teachers is also important. Prayer will not only make a difference for the teachers and other volunteers, but you will change as you pray for them. Use this chart to center your prayers on those in ministry with you.

Sunday	Monday	Tuesday	Wednesday	Thursday	Friday	Saturday
Pray for our education program and all those who work with it.	(list 1/5 volunteers)	(list 1/5 volunteers)	(list 1/5 volunteers)	(list 1/5 volunteers)	(list 1/5 volunteers)	Pray for my relationship to our volunteers and my growth as a leader.

---

1. Delia Halverson, *How to Train Volunteer Teachers* (Nashville: Abingdon Press, 1991) p. 11.

What About Yourself?

The broad scope of Christian education can be mind-boggling and stressful. If for no other reason than that, anyone in the career needs to take time for self. But there is more reason for being aware of self in this career. We must recognize our need for spiritual development too.

Your Spiritual Personality

Knowing your own spiritual personality will help you to know how to deepen your spiritual life. Recently we have recognized that a person's personality plays a key role in the way that he or she grows spiritually. While research in this area continues, evidence already exists of which we should take note.

No doubt you know of people who seem to grow deeper spiritually even though they seldom spend time alone, and others who absolutely must have some alone time. Our spiritual search is an inward journey where we recognize the reality and mystery of God. It is a personal experience, and the paths we choose to travel may differ. For some people it may be in private, and for others it may come through interaction with other people, reflecting on the experiences of the world and their meaning and significance. Some people may need to withdraw, while for others the spiritual journey comes through involvement in the world.

Malcolm Goldsmith, in *Knowing Me, Knowing God,* uses the Myers-Briggs personality test to explore spirituality. The book features a questionnaire that helps individuals examine how different aspects of spiritual growth are influenced by their personality.

Spiritual Personality Summary of Persons with:

Sensing spirituality

• take in information through their senses.

• music, speaking, and silence are important to them, as are touch, and smell, and taste.

• concerned with specifics and with the "here and now," what is happening today in the circumstances of life rather than vague, generalized plans about the future.

• want to cut out words and ideas and see spirituality in the simplest form.

• "Don't talk about it, show me!"[1]

iNtuitive spirituality

• take in information through their imagination.

• future-oriented, aware of possibilities, living in a provisional world, looking and hoping for a new and better situation.

- concerned with the "big picture" rather than details.
- quickly become bored with repetition, practicalities, and the minutiae of plans and present circumstances.
- attracted to a theology that places stress on the reign of God bringing about justice and peace.
- God is so mysterious and wonderful that words to describe God become meaningless.
- receive as much insight into the workings of God by reading novels as they do from reading the Bible.
- scripture is likely to be used as a launching-off point for reflective thought about issues, expecting that God will use that Bible passage to bring other things to mind.[2]

Feeling spirituality
- think that decisions are good if they take other people into account, and they will put themselves out for the sake of others.
- place themselves in other people's shoes and enjoy helping others.
- prize peace and harmony and go to considerable lengths to create such conditions, often at personal expense or inconvenience.
- often turn a blind eye to things which ought to be challenged or to people who need to be confronted.
- identify with gospel images and situations: sacrificial victim, turning the other cheek, going the extra mile, and bearing the suffering of others. It is almost as though it is more Christlike to be hurt.
- sometimes an unconscious desire to be exploited or "put upon," interpreted as a sign of authentic discipleship.
- commitment to a church community is important, getting to know people in order to discover their needs and troubles and provide strength. [3]

Thinking spirituality
("Thinking" in a technical sense, not to imply that those who prefer the Feeling function are non-thinkers)
- God is perceived as being primarily righteous, just, faithful, true, consistent, wise, and reasonable (not offending reason).
- truth is truth and cannot be molded or twisted to suit circumstances or to avoid giving offense.
- firm, logical, cool, and analytical spirituality.
- can be assertive, critical, adversarial, distant, and impersonal.

- stewards of creation, responsible and concerned about truth and justice.
- God makes demands on our lives, requiring us to live with integrity and to seek righteousness and freedom.
- like objectivity and exactness.
- like public worship to be done decently and with order.
- tend not to like their privacy being invaded, especially if they are also introverts.
- the very process of thinking can be a form of spiritual exercise and an offering to God.
- may question prayers and hymns, checking out their words to see if they are logical, consistent, or true.[4]

Sabbath Time

I recall, as a child, the special day each week when we drove out of town a few miles and spent two to three hours at a friend's home. In fact, sometimes we never went inside the house and didn't even see our friends. These friends owned a log home near the Hillsborough River, with acres of woods and creeks to roam. There was a large lawn with a picnic table and a tall swing that swung out over a creek. The swing was so tall that the fire department had to replace the rope. My mother had an understanding with them that we could use their property each Saturday whether they were home or not. It was our own, private getaway.

My dad was a preacher, and at that time we lived in Ybor City, a very congested area of Tampa. The streets were brick, and the cars rattled along one side of our house as the streetcar clanged its way up and down another street not a half block away. We were less than three blocks from the busiest street in town; and within a block was one of many cigar factories in the neighborhood, all of which used whistles to signal their workers when their work or their lunch hours began or ended. On Saturday nights the Cuban Club, just a block in the other direction, opened its doors and windows and pumped up the band. To top it off, our parsonage was attached to the church, quite literally! Two of our three outside doors opened directly into a fellowship hall and classroom corridor. There was no way of escaping Dad's work, twenty-four hours a day, seven days a week, without physically removing ourselves from the premises. And my wise mother saw to it that we did just that.

Most people grew up with a legalistic view of the Sabbath rest on Sundays, and they either accepted it wholeheartedly or scoffed at the idea. The fact that preachers worked on Sundays did not automatically warrant them another day as Sabbath. The only Sabbath we knew was Sunday. However, that is not a true understanding of Sabbath. We are made with a rhythm in our bodies just as the world is made with rhythm. And, as Jesus said, the Sabbath is made for us. That rhythm involves rest. I often remind folks, as we close an intensive meeting or training and head to bed, that God could have made our bodies so that they did not require sleep. So sleep is a gift from God. The same is true for the rhythm of work and rest. The Hebrew people discovered this even before they discovered writing, and so the Sabbath was established.

Folks who work with the church can easily spend all of our time teaching and preaching about the Sabbath, but never learning to incorporate it into our own lives. Sunday is a working day for us, one of the most demanding days of the week. Consequently, we must take another day as our Sabbath, our cycle of rest.

There are several aspects of the Sabbath that are important to our well-being.

• *First there is the aspect of worship.* Although we as church employees worship on Sundays with the congregation, we also need some type of worship that is simply "looking and loving" God. Often our responsibility for Sunday worships and all that is happening in and around those worship hours makes it difficult for us to completely let go of our surroundings and be able to dwell in the embracing love of God. So we must find another time to worship in that manner.

• *Then there is the aspect of work.* The cycle of rest from work may be different for us than it is for the farmer or the carpenter who is physically active every day. Our rest from mental and emotional stress may come in the form of digging in the garden or paddling a canoe. But the rhythm is not complete without rest from work.

• *Another important aspect of the Sabbath is a new approach to life.* Our world is so work or production driven that we do not recognize the importance of community, of simply enjoying the fellowship of others with no driven need to produce. Society impresses upon us the importance of producing a product, or money, or even a winning score in a softball game. If we have nothing to show for our time, then we feel that it's been squandered. But a part of the rhythm of life is simply enjoying others. I was once asked to recall one of the happiest times of my life, when I felt pleasantly and peacefully happy but not exuberantly happy. My mind went back to a time when I was sitting on the back porch with my children and my husband, simply enjoying the spring sunshine with no special agenda. Those of us in church leadership also need the Sabbath of relationships with people who are not in our particular church. This gives us a new perspective.

We must take inventory of our Sabbaths periodically and rebuild the true meaning of the day. When was the last time that you took a true Sabbath?

Spiritual Retreats and Quiet Times, Planned and Found

My mother must have had an ancestral relationship with John Wesley, because she awakened very early each morning and spent time reading and in prayer before the rest of the house stirred. Even though I'm basically a morning person, I have difficulty getting up before the sun comes up. And I must admit that I cannot be habitual about the discipline of reading scripture and prayer for a short time each day. I've found that I become frustrated when the thirty or forty-five minutes are over and

I'm still enjoying my quiet time. So I find it more beneficial to set aside longer periods of time at other times during the week for this type of study and prayer. However, I have found that there are many opportunities throughout each day to catch a glimpse of the Power we call God. And those "found" times act to recharge me throughout my busy day.

These glimpses come while watching a butterfly light on a flower outside my window, or stopping long enough to hear the pounding of the rain on the roof. Or as I close the blinds, head for bed, when I step into the moonlight that splatters across the floor. Or at a time I watch a child smile as he hands another child his toy. Another might come during the moment of thanks when the doctor tells my husband he can leave the hospital. Or even the times when I stop gulping my food and slowly chew, savoring the flavor of the most delicious halibut I've ever eaten.

Without these planned and found times of retreat and spiritual awakening, we become hollow. Some people never seek such times. However, these times are ours to be cherished. Don't let them slip past as you gallop through life.

Prepare for Prayer

No one can tell you the best way to pray. Each person must find ways that suit him or her best. If you do not have a pattern for your personal time with God, consider the following and adapt it to your own needs.

P *repare yourself.* Find a location that is comfortable and where you will not be disturbed.

R *epeat a simple verse* or prayer. Learn a short Bible verse or prayer or song. Breathe slowly for several seconds, being conscious of your breathing, and then repeat the verse or prayer or sing the song quietly. You might try 1 Timothy 1:2*b* or a verse from Psalms, perhaps 8:1*a* or 46:10. Or sing "Spirit of the Living God" or pray Brother Lawrence's prayer, "Lord, make me according to thy heart."

A *ccept God into your heart.* To do this, center into the very heart of you. Consider the part of you that feels love, that feels sadness, the part that is happy when you do for others. Then ask God to come into that part of you.

Y *ield all that bothers you to God.* Whatever is trou-

bling you, turn it over to God. Know that God understands your problems.

E *njoy God's presence.* Just spend some time "looking and loving" God. Relax in the joy of being loved by God. Feel God's strength and peace.

R *eview how you felt.* Begin a prayer journal, writing down some of the feelings and thoughts that came to you as you prayed. Writing it down makes your feelings and thoughts more concrete.[5]

Journaling

Journaling has become a more common term than in years past. Yet I often hear the phrase, "Journaling isn't for everyone." Perhaps, we should simply say everyone doesn't journal in the same manner. What works for me or someone else, may not work for you. Some folks journal without even realizing that is what they are doing it. The act of journaling is not producing a written manuscript, but rather a process of reflection. My husband

seldom writes them down, but he often comes up with four-line rhymes that reflect his thought processing. I journal using a notebook, but sometimes I go several weeks without writing anything in it. I tried journaling with the computer, but found it too much like work. A friend with whom I sometimes worship writes thoughts in her notebook many times during a day.

If you would like to try journaling with the written word, here are some suggestions:

• Divide your notebook (I use a loose leaf notebook) into three sections:

Subject: In this section you will label different pages according to a particular subject. My notebook has alphabetized pages for God, heaven, love, nature, peace, and so on. When you are reflecting on a particular subject, write it in this section. If you are writing in the dated or scripture section of your journal and recognize that you are covering a specific subject, then turn to this section and record a reference to the particular date or scripture where the thoughts are recorded.

Scripture: If you are reading a scripture and certain thoughts come to mind, record them on the pages in this section. I make up a page as I need it and label it by the particular book in the Bible. The only exception to this is that I create separate pages for each psalm that I reflect on. The pages in this section are arranged in biblical order. As you work with this section, when you recognize that a passage covers a specific subject, turn to the subject section of your notebook and make a notation on the appropriate page to also look in the scripture section for this text.

Date: Write general reflections you have under the day's date. If it refers to a certain subject, turn to the subject section of your notebook and make reference to the date where you have recorded your thoughts for future reference. Don't record dates in this section ahead of time, because you may not journal every day. The date is simply for cross reference purposes, not for keeping an account of how often you write in your journal.

• When your notebook becomes too full, take out several pages and file them according to date, subject, and scripture. This method has been particularly helpful as I've prepared keynote addresses or written articles on certain subjects. It also acts as a review of how my faith has matured through the years. My faith journey is personal and kept private, except in the ways that I wish to share it with others.

A Spirit Journey by Anne Broyles (see Resources and References) offers the best introduction to journaling, and offers helps and places to practice journaling through events, scripture, guided meditations, dreams, literature, and conversations.

Covenant/Support Groups

During a recent conversation with a Christian educator who maintains a busy schedule, I asked, "When have you had your Sabbath this week?" Some people may have felt that I was intruding, or hovering over a younger educator like a mother hen; however, this young woman recognized my question as concern for her health, both physical and spiritual.

Covenant and support groups are important for your well-being as well as your career development. A support group might consist of several Christian educators who meet on a regular basis, while a covenant group calls for a bit more commitment. But the commitment is well worth it, because in a covenant group you promise to look out for the well-being of each other. Covenant groups are generally intimate gatherings of three or four persons, who perhaps meet for an hour on a specific morning each week. The group may not even include other Christian educators, but the members are concerned about one another and hold each other accountable. Participants typically share with their small group their dreams and goals, and receive help in striving to reach those goals. *Covenant Discipleship* by David Lowes Watson provides a more detailed understanding of covenant groups.

For information about career support groups, contact your denominational office. Some groups are multidenominational. I belong to Christian Educator's Fellowship, which is sponsored by the United Methodist Church but includes members from many denominations. See Resources and References for information about other groups. Most have state or local chapters with which you can meet on a regular basis.

Even if joining a national organization is not an option, you would do well to contact other churches in your immediate area and find out who is in charge of Christian education in their congregations. Plan an occasional gathering with these individuals. The group in my community meets once a month for lunch either at a church or a local restaurant. Although we have no specific agenda, I always come away with new ideas and a renewed energy to carry on my ministry.

Continuing Education

When it was first suggested that I write this book, I was hesitant because I did not want people to think that all that they needed to know about Christian education could be found in this or any other book. The profession of Christian education is always changing. Even though the final two years of my undergraduate study were concentrated in Christian education, I have continued to take classes and other short-term studies whenever possible. But now I realize that I would have grown much more, and at a much faster pace, had I concentrated more on theological studies. Christian education is a balance of practice and theory, everyday life and biblical study, as well as common sense and theological reflection. You can never get enough continuing education.

Most denominations offer a certification process that requires a certain amount of education and experience. Explore these opportunities. Such certification creates a professional attitude about your career and usually leads to better ministry opportunities with churches that respect and value your leadership gifts. But more important, certification does two additional things. It directs your ongoing education and affirms the fact that you see your career as a calling from God, to be certified or commissioned by the church.

Schedules and Lifestyles

Some twenty years ago Christian educators balked at maintaining flexible office hours. In fact, many simply declared that they would hold firm office hours and would not be available for night meetings more than one or two nights per week. Perhaps such a move was necessary to give some credibility to the profession, but it was not very practical.

In most cases, we work with volunteers who hold full-time jobs, so we must have flexible hours to accommodate them. Part-time church jobs usually mean full-time hours, and full-time jobs generally mean time-and-a-half. However, we do not need to put ourselves on twenty-four hour schedules. Make a habit of requesting comp time for the extra hours spent on multiple night meetings and overnight retreats. When you come into the office late or take the afternoon off in order to compensate for the extra hours, let the office staff know the circumstances. You may feel that your schedule is of no concern to others, but we must recognize that the office staff are the ones who face the public, and most people are accustomed to strict office hours. However, it is best to establish the hours when you expect to be in the office so that your volunteers will know the best times to talk with you.

Do your church and yourself a service by periodically keeping a week's record of the tasks you performed or completed. Break each day into fifteen-minute increments. One church hired me as their first full-time Christian educator. After I'd been on the job for about a year, several council members questioned whether the job should be full time. Obviously they were unaware of the evening meetings that I attended or the phone calls I had to make from home at night, or even the amount of prep time that was necessary for some of the programs. When I kept a record of my activities for a full week and tallied up the amount of hours on the phone, filing articles, or preparing for a workshop, they were surprised. As was I. I knew I was working forty hours a week, but what I didn't realize was that I was working more than forty hours a week! I discovered that I was doing some work that could easily be done by someone with no Christian education background, such as collecting supplies for a workshop or filing articles for teachers. As the job expanded, I found that by asking for a secretary with organizational skills I was able to accomplish twice as much. This was good stewardship of my time and of the church's money.

The best thing that you can do for your emotional and physical health is to work constantly at simplifying your life. No one can tell you exactly how to do this, but aligning your life with God will make your life simple, even if it is busy. This does not mean that God's will for your life is to do everything that someone in the church asks you to do! Your understanding of God's will for you is something that you must determine for yourself in each situation. Perhaps this quote from *Living Simply*, will help:

In Micah 6:8 we read that God has told us what is good and required of us: to do justice, to love kindness, and to walk humbly with God. Although we are made in God's image, as humans we still need some practical applications to get started. Here are a few suggestions. As we use them, we must continue to seek to align ourselves with God.

• Keep your eye on the task instead of the results.

• Never make a major decision without allowing a certain number of hours or days for reflection and prayer.

• On a card, list six items or write a sentence of what is most important to you. Carry the card with you and refer to it when making decisions.

• Make decisions ahead of time concerning such things as budgets, gifts to charities, type of job you will seek, social choices you will make, and appropriate use of time.

• Recognize the difference between concern and anxiety.

• See prayer as a process for change in yourself instead of a formula for a product (a means of getting what you want).

• Own your talents and where they can be used, and leave other situations to the talents God has given others.

• Take pride in your call from God. Recognize that humility, humus and human come from a common root word. In humility we offer ourselves to be used and refashioned by God.

• Make your decision to the best of your ability and then own that decision and move forward instead of wondering if you were right. The time of absolute certainty never comes.

God has made us complex. What a joy that we are complex and not merely puppets. To simplify we must choose to develop the character of God in our own lives. God gave us choice, and we must use that choice to line ourselves up with God's will. Soren Kierkegaard wrote in his book, *Purity of Heart Is to Will One Thing*, "I am, therefore I must decide." When I line myself up with God I can decide what to strip away, how to use my time, what to purchase with my money, and just how to live my life.[6]

Your Job

After I had been on staff in a church for about eighteen months, it dawned on me that I had not met with the personnel committee. I had met from time to time with my staff supervisor, but I felt that the committee needed to be aware of what I was doing from my own mouth. I did not want a problem or conflict to arise and then realize that I'd never even sat across from these folks and looked them in the eye. So I asked for an opportunity to talk with them. Your relationship with your hiring committee is of prime importance. Take every opportunity to get to know them personally. Be sure that they are aware of your work by keeping them well informed. If your church does not assign an individual from the committee to each staff member, request to be assigned to someone or get to know one of the members who can represent you when the committee meets. This person could also approach you with concerns that the committee has about your ministry that require your attention.

For example, there were no job descriptions for the first few staff positions that I held. After floundering for a few months, I sought out other Christian educators and asked for copies of their job descriptions. Then I launched into writing my own. Since then, I have come to recognize the importance of the church taking ownership in creating a job description. I do feel, however, that it is important for the education committee, or the governing group of the church that works with the Christian educator, to take the primary lead in creating the job description. Their suggestions can be passed on to the personnel or staff-parish committee for approval. The following is a format I find helpful in working with staff job descriptions. In addition, a sample mission description for a Director of Christian Education can be found in appendix 20.

Considerations When Preparing a Staff Job Description

Review Deuteronomy 31:12.

Pray for God's guidance.

Review baptismal vows. Talk about the importance of carrying on the faith and the fact that every job in a church, no matter what, contributes to that goal.

Look at:

Congregation	Ages and family makeup
	Theological makeup
Community	Ages and family
	Mobility
	Other resources/groups

Look at your church's mission description and see how this job carries out a part of that mission.

Look at current program and how all jobs fit together. How does this job you're considering affect others?

What materials/supplies/curriculum will be used in this position?

Look at short-term dreams for this position and then any wild dreams.

Look at present staff (paid and volunteer), their responsibilities, and how they relate to this position.

Consider the needs this person will meet.

Look at the physical location where the person will work and the resources that are available.

What training and continuing education will you offer?

What budget will the person work with?

Consider the responsibility you want the person to have to his or her personal devotional and family life. Include this in the description.

Write up the final form of the description, then offer a prayer of thanks for this ministry.

1. Malcolm Goldsmith, *Knowing Me, Knowing God* (Nashville: Abingdon Press, 1997), pp. 57-58.
2. Ibid., pp. 64, 66.
3. Ibid., pp. 72, 74.
4. Ibid., pp. 76-78.
5. Delia Halverson, "Teach Me How to Pray," *Youth!* magazine (February, 1990).
6. Halverson, *Living Simply* (Nashville: Abingdon Press, 1996), pp. 23-24.

A Final Word

Since my ministry is primarily to help other Christian education teachers and leaders, I encourage communication from you. If there are ideas within these pages you would like to discuss further, or if you have a question not covered here, feel free to contact me. I'm also interested in learning how this book, or any of my other books, have helped you in your ministry. Please contact me directly at:

Delia Halverson

Faith Discovery Ministries
15286 Cricket Lane
Fort Myers, FL 33919
941-432-0952
samandee@compuserve.com

I can also be reached through:

Abingdon Press
or
Christian Educator's Fellowship
PO Box 24930
Nashville, TN 37202

615-749-6870

Adult Generations

Generation Xers **adults may be like this:**
- born during the sixties, seventies, and early eighties
- also called the 13th Generation (13th generation of American citizens), Baby Busters (numbers of births down) and the Lost or Gap Generation
- born of parents who looked out for #1 and had no firm religious convictions
- products of contraceptives, two-income families, changing sex roles, limited resources, violent models, mobile lifestyles, declining job markets
- from homes of plenty, but many from homes below poverty level
- a generation with median income of $10,000, many without jobs
- expected to have greatest impact on money and marketplace

Characteristics of Generation Xers are:
- independent, view themselves as realists and survivors, risk takers
- skeptic of people: let down by national role figures they admired
- flexible, anxious to cut to the action without wasting time talking
- work at jobs to enjoy leisure and expect to have several careers in life
- slow to commitment to marriage and raising children but hope for stable family life
- good at finding alternative ways around impossible situations

Generation Xers want from a church:
- redefinition of Christian value: life can be abundant without abundance
- willing to listen and offer understanding, encouraging them to seek their *own* answers and make *own* decisions
- pragmatic Christianity, including ALL of life
- involvement of laity in experiential study, worship leadership, and decisions with action
- biblical emphasis on survival during hardships
- experiential learning with practical applications to any spiritual decisions
- opportunity for hands-on mission to persons *before* learning about Christ
- discussions *after* doing or after active learning experiences
- action rather than polite conversation about ideologies
- multiple worship styles involving senses and time frames
- small support groups, styles and locations for study, service to others, leadership opportunities
- images of diversity of God

Baby Boomers **adults may be like this:**
- born between mid forties and mid sixties

- one in three Americans
- have 3-D lifestyle: Delayed marriage; Deferred childbearing; Divorcing couples
- often dictate change because of their sheer numbers
- not all swinging and rich: many average $15,000 or less income
- generally unchurched and biblically illiterate
- baptized as infants
- few joined a church
- questioning, as they enter midlife

Characteristics of Baby Boomers are:
- two-income families
- moms pulled between moving up in career and family devotion
- dads more involved with children
- materialistic models—peer pressure
- no dedication to one denomination or church
- tight schedules

Baby Boomers want in a church:
- innovative worship
- involvement *before* joining
- family involvement
- consideration of pressed and erratic time schedules (suppers, babysitting, meeting times clustered, etc.)
- short-term assignments and studies
- options provided
- opportunity to develop common bonds, support systems
- because of limited time, want their time to be useful, not just filled
- opportunity to help in an area of their interest
- evidence that their commitment makes a difference
- service that is people, rather than task, oriented
- awareness and help to oppressed, mission support (money and hands-on)
- support of global peace
- more than informational Bible study, affecting their lives

Silent Generation adults may be like this:
- born mid twenties to mid forties
- raised in depression/war
- born too soon or too late
- early marriage/childbearing
- dilemma over feminism
- personal (not national) passages

Characteristics of the Silent Generation are:
- arbitrator/mediator
- adaptive but slow decisions
- directed to others
- assisting roles/public life
- like to deliberate
- gather facts/opinions
- prefer process to outcome

The Silent Generation wants in the church:

- advocacy opportunities
- time to reflect before decisions
- help with life situations
- discussion opportunities
- praise for leadership
- change with reason
- people-oriented service

GI Generation adults may be like this:

- born before mid twenties
- horse/buggy to space travel
- two world wars, plus
- one-income families
- strong civic/government involvement

Characteristics of the GI Generation are:

- self-sufficient, aggressive
- strong values
- powerful work ethic
- believe in institutions
- strong denomination ties
- resist change

GI Generation wants in the church:

- belonging in community
- loyalty
- ownership/own space
- strong Bible study
- emphasis on values
- consistent traditions
- attention to detail[1]

---

1. Delia Halverson, *Leading Adult Learners* (Nashville: Abingdon Press, 1995), p. 24.

Characteristics of Children and Youth

The Infant **may be like this:**
- wiggles, squirms, squeals, and kicks—grasps for items.
- smiles for strangers as well as family.
- crawls or rolls from one place to another.
- responds in individual ways.

The infant needs:
- to be loved and cared for and kept dry and changed.
- an environment that is safe and clean (and nontoxic).
- adults who recognize the child's behavior and offer encouragement.
- room for crawling and objects to hold and grasp.
- items to watch and follow with eyes.

Parents of infants need:
- to know the environment is clean and safe and the child is cared for and loved.
- to be called by name and recognized.
- to know that you have concern when the child is ill.
- to be assured that the child's interest is yours.

The Toddler and Two-Year-Old **may be like this:**
- beginning to know the power of saying "no."
- fearless in trying new things.
- climbing, stepping on, to get where he wants to be.
- begins to match words with objects.
- toddler has special language of own; two-year-old beginning to drop it.
- unable to comprehend pronouns (Jimmy kick the ball instead of "I").
- may hit or attack peers when cannot communicate with words.
- plays well beside instead of with others; everything is "me" centered.
- very short attention span.

Two-year-old particularly:
- has beginning capabilities of some creative activities.
- often prefers adult relationships to peer.
- can recall events of yesterday, missing toys, and so forth.
- uses color names but unable to identify yet.
- uses number words to accompany serial pointing, foundation for later discriminative counting.
- talks while acts and acts while talks.

- can't fold paper well yet, but enjoys using paper.
- begins process thinking (pushes chair to climb up to get something).
- growing sense of possession displayed by hiding toys to have later.
- shows off to adults and peers to make them laugh.
- shows affection spontaneously.
- mimics adult expressions of emotion.
- dawdles often.
- considers self "older" than younger child.

The toddler and two-year-old need:
- adults who keep constant check on actions and offer comfort.
- routine to give them stability.
- adults who do first, and then explain as they do it again.
- room to move about and have individual play.
- motion activities to satisfy muscular development.
- to hear others tell stories about him/herself and familiar belongings.
- listeners and encouragement in developing communication skills.
- help with words to show emotions. "You are *angry* because..."
- opportunity to express possessiveness.
- pictures at their eye level, 2 or 3 feet above floor and low shelves within reach.
- songs and games with repetition and imitation.
- multiple toys where possible for along-side play; nontoxic materials.
- nearby bathroom facilities for two-year-olds.
- opportunity to see creative accomplishment for two-year-olds.

Parents of toddlers and two-year-olds need:
- to know that the environment is clean and safe and child cared for and loved.
- to be called by name and recognized.
- to know that you have concern when the child is ill.
- to become involved with child's class.
- to be assured child's interest is yours and you love him or her even when there are problems.

The Three-Year-Old **may be like this:**
- enjoys motor activity, but less than twos.
- enjoys finger manipulations with play materials.
- likes to use crayons but unable to stay in lines well.
- drawing more directed with some controlled marks (not enough to draw person).
- delight in scissors. Begin cutting "fringes" around edges of paper and then cutting across paper. Cutting out pictures comes with more practice.
- has longer attention span.
- builds tower of 9 to 10 blocks.
- folds paper lengthwise and crosswise, but not diagonally.
- can pedal, jump upward, balances on one foot for short time.
- starts and stops easily and makes sharp turns.

- begins to recognize forms.
- sometimes rather tidy and orderly.
- sentences becoming longer and many questions.
- words now instruments for relating ideas, concepts, relationships, and so forth.
- enjoys creating chants.
- tries to use muscles to solve problem instead of thinking ability. (Will try to force puzzle piece instead of thinking to turn around.)
- has sense of incompleteness, fragments (turn page, and so forth).
- beginning classification, comparing things.
- learning to listen but still enjoys being listened to.
- beginning bargaining ability—sacrificing something now for later.
- strong desire to please.
- talks to self and imaginary persons.
- enjoys other children, but still needs solitary/parallel play.
- beginning understanding of waiting turns and sharing.
- may ask questions to which already knows answer.

The three-year-old needs:
- beginning finger plays.
- simple rhythm instrument opportunities (may be homemade).
- to watch forms being drawn to imitate.
- opportunities to "do it myself."
- materials for development of smaller muscles, along with some big muscle.
- adults sensitive to inner feelings, who may cover embarrassment.
- appreciation for contributions to community living.
- understanding tolerance and acceptance of different development levels.
- understanding of the unknown and what causes things.
- modeling of Christian values.

Parents of three-year-olds need:
- to be called by name and recognized.
- to know that you have concern when the child is ill.
- to know that the environment is clean and safe.
- to know that the child is cared for and loved.
- to become involved with child's class.
- to be assured the child's interest is yours and you love even when problems.
- encouragement when their child develops differently from another.

The Four-Year-Old **may be like this:**
- runs, stops, turns with ease.
- may be able to skip and stand on one leg for a period of time.
- throws and catches ball or bean bag; swings by self.
- can recognize and reproduce body movements.
- strings large and small beads (not very small) and follow simple patterns.
- copies circle, triangle, square; matches colors and shapes.

- claps hands in imitation of simple rhythm.
- can use brushes at easel properly.
- cuts on straight line and some simple outlines; simple paper folding.
- recognizes simple alike and different objects.
- identifies missing parts if not too complex.
- memory is developing for 2-4 color/object sequence.
- recognizes own name; knows first and last name.
- recognizes and matches various environmental sounds.
- retells very short stories accurately; recalls jingles, rhymes, and so forth.
- using language, communicates needs and begins to solve problems.
- little comprehension of past and future.
- literal thinking; baffled by story-teller analogies.
- worships God, although cannot verbally explain (in awe of creation).
- likes to go from one thing to another rather than repeat.
- constant questioning; much chattering (sometimes for attention).
- more bossy and mature than threes, but enjoys groups of 2-3 children.
- shares possessions and suggests turns, but does not play orderly.

The four-year-old needs:
- simple rhythm instrument opportunities (may be homemade).
- opportunities to "do it myself."
- adults sensitive to inner feelings, who may cover embarrassment.
- appreciation for contributions to community living.
- understanding tolerance and acceptance of different development levels.
- understanding of the unknown and what causes things.
- modeling of Christian values.
- opportunities to extend social development.
- persons who talk literally.
- frequent opportunities to move about without undue pressure.
- opportunities for quiet reflection.

Parents of four-year-olds need:
- to be called by name and recognized.
- to know that you have concern when the child is ill.
- to know that the environment is clean and safe.
- to know that the child is cared for and loved.
- to become involved with child's class.
- to be assured child's interest is yours and you love even when problems.
- encouragement to follow up on class activities at home.

The Five-Year-Old may be like this:
- actively going most of time, but fatigues quickly.
- better developed in large muscles; becoming better in small muscles.
- slower physical growth than previous years.
- responds to routine and organization with some interest in organized games.

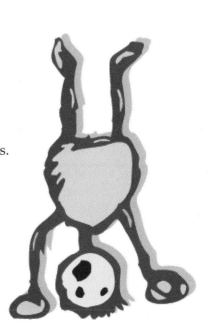

- plans and plays together in small groups.
- incomplete eye development (often far-sighted).
- left or right-handedness usually established.
- handles personal needs (dressing within limits, eating, toilet, and so forth).
- jealous of other children; competes for adult attention.
- strong link to parents, particularly mother; may return to younger behavior.
- begins to look for reason for authority.
- developing sense of humor.
- becoming cooperative and helpful, but will argue and become angry.
- enjoys small responsibilities and thrives on praise and affection.
- copies authority figures in play (parents, teacher, and so forth).
- expects rules and limits to be literal; sometimes confuses fact and fantasy.
- better understanding of sequence of events but little concept of time.
- developing respect for rights of others.
- little understanding of cause and effect.
- "special" friend, or feels left out because has no "special" friend.

The five-year-old needs:
- simple answers to the many questions asked.
- first-hand experiences to gain new information.
- simple opportunities to make generalizations and see relationships.
- guidance in new skill of making thoughtful decisions.
- adults sensitive to inner feelings, and who may cover embarrassment.
- praise of accomplishments and contributions to group living.
- modeling of Christian values.
- persons who talk literally instead of abstractly.
- opportunities for quiet reflection.
- to be recognized by teacher in community (at grocery store, and so forth).
- to feel needed, with assigned "helper/steward" or leader positions.
- activities that involve the senses.
- people who will listen with ears and eyes.
- changes in pace—active followed by quiet.

Parents of five-year-olds need:
- to be called by name and recognized.
- to know that you have concern when the child is ill.
- to know that the child is cared for and loved.
- encouragement when their child develops differently from another.
- to become involved with child's class.
- to be assured child's interest is yours and you love even when problems.
- encouragement to follow up on class activities at home.

The Younger Elementary Boy or Girl may be like this:
- restless, active, and energetic but still tire easily.
- experience slow physical development as body growth stabilizes.
- less interest in own body as physical being; not yet conscious of sexual being.
- likes to learn by doing.
- discouraged if unable to complete a project because of time or skill.

- math skills improving, but still need concrete terms.
- by grade three beginning map reading skills and understand some history.
- by second grade beginning cursive writing.
- attention span of 10-15 minutes.
- beginning to manipulate symbols in mind without use of hands or objects.
- beginning to read, but reading at different levels.
- begin reasoning from own experience.
- rule-bound (everything right or wrong; "fair" means "equal").
- reasoning skill increasing.
- reflects parental attitudes.
- vivid imagination and enjoy dramatization.
- like stories, read to or to read themselves.
- "me-ism" develops toward others. (God loves me —I love others).
- interests of boys and girls often differ.
- enjoys "best friend" but may shift friends; peer cliques/clubs shift easily.

The younger elementary boy or girl needs:
- "real" tools and equipment rather than toys.
- opportunities to be with people of all ages and playmates of both sexes.
- opportunities to explore meaning of Bible stories to own life.
- opportunities to use art forms and words to convey ideas and feelings.
- simple interpretation of symbols although young one may not grasp it.
- pride of owning "own" Bible and help in learning to use it.
- opportunity to do own planning and solve own problems.
- conversation, songs, and stories to help them learn some Bible verses.
- free dramatic play and spontaneous dramatization.
- adults who point out child's positive physical and personality characteristics.
- sympathy when emotionally hurt but encouragement to forget quickly.
- projects broken down into small tasks and understanding when s/he attempts things beyond ability and fails.
- experiences with lifecycles and relating these to God as creator.
- encouragement to ask "how" and "why" although generally accept most everything told about God.
- opportunities for quiet reflection.

Parents of younger elementary children need:
- to be called by name and recognized.
- to know that you have concern when the child is ill.
- to prepare for child's loyalty to switch from parents to peers.
- to become involved with child's class.
- to be assured child's interest is yours and you love even when problems.
- encouragement to follow up on class activities at home.

The Older Elementary Boy or Girl **may be like this:**
- increasingly interested in peer group, in forming "clubs" and "gangs." Looking to peers for authority more than adults. Tending to accept without question the values of the group.
- growing interest, especially among girls, in the opposite sex. Many, especially boys, may continue to prefer activities with own sex.
- increasing independence, wanting to make own decisions.

- interested in perfecting skills.
- experiencing a spurt in growth, especially in girls. May feel awkward, gawky, embarrassed. Late growers may be anxious, be called "Shrimp," "Tiny," and so forth.
- thinking about what he/she will do what grows up.
- increasingly able to think abstractly, to reason, to grasp the relation of cause and effect.
- skeptical, questioning about matters of faith accepted earlier.
- feeling intensely about fair play and justice.
- informed and concerned about people and conditions around the world.
- increased attention span (15-20 minutes).

The older elementary boy or girl needs:
- many wholesome, meaningful activities in a group in which he/she has a sense of belonging.
- encouragement to do things with individuals and group whose values are desirable, to develop independently his/her own set of values.
- opportunity to make own decisions where appropriate, to share in determining plans and procedures of own church group.
- adults who expect the best he or she is able to produce, who provide opportunity to master skills in which the child shows interest.
- adults who help the child understand/accept individual growth "time tables."
- opportunity to explore many possible occupations, to develop a sense of Christian vocation (direction of life) used later in deciding about occupation.
- encouragement to express honest skepticism. Adults who affirm their own faith, help children do their own thinking, and do not expect them to believe as they themselves believe.
- adults who are fair and just in their relations with others, who help boys and girls see the implications of their faith for their personal and social relations.
- opportunity to engage directly and indirectly in the worldwide ministry of their church.
- opportunity to worship, learn, and play with persons of all ages.

Parents of older elementary children need:
- to be called by name and recognized.
- to know that you have concern when the child is ill.
- understanding that children are transferring allegiance from adults to peers.
- understanding that inquiring into our faith is a natural development process.
- to become involved with child's class.
- to be assured child's interest is yours and you love even when problems.
- encouragement to follow up on class activities at home.

The Middle Schooler **may be like this:**
- varying developmental changes. Some develop more rapidly than others. Those on the leading edge sometimes feel ahead, and those who change less rapidly feel inadequate.
- usually experience a sudden growth spurt in height. When this happens faster in girls than in boys it causes great differences in the sexes.
- awkwardness as they learn to handle bigger hands, feet, shoulders, hips.
- unaware of the increase in physical strength.
- great need to look "like" peers. Attractiveness is of great concern.
- experimenting with various roles, personalities, values, and so forth.

- trying to break away from parental ties and develop peer ties.
- anxiety over personal identity.
- fluctuating between lack of self-esteem and good self-esteem.
- moving from concrete thought into more general, abstract, and symbolic thought. But some still think concretely.
- reading levels vary greatly.
- most have short attention span/many learn better through electronic media.
- feeling isolated with little ability to communicate.
- vacillate between dependence and independence.
- moving from using rules only for own purpose and concrete punishment, to recognizing that our roles and action affect everyone.
- questioning the literal faith of childhood and accepting conventional faith.
- religious knowledge minimal and poorly organized.

The middle schooler needs:
- many and varied learning opportunities that are active and gamelike.
- opportunity to choose activities, whether to read, and so forth.
- studies and programs that deal with *their* everyday problems.
- opportunity to engage directly and indirectly in the worldwide ministry of their church.
- adults who don't play favorites and talk to everyone in group.
- adults who will not embarrass them in front of others.
- adults who set an example of not making fun of other people.
- adults who ask "What do you think?" and really listen and accept answer.
- encouragement in new thought process.
- affirmation when they have accomplished something.
- recognition when encountered in the community.
- persons who will listen without "offering advice" unless asked, and then it's better to help the middle schooler come up with own answers.
- adults who share their own beliefs, but do not force it upon them.
- opportunities to develop a real sense of belonging to the group.

Parents of middle schoolers need:
- to know just what's happening and when.
- to know that their child is under constant supervision.
- to have regular opportunities for discussion with leaders.
- help in understanding their middle schooler.
- opportunity to be a part of the program.

The High Schooler **may be like this:**
- questioning whether they want to be individuals or part of the crowd.
- individually different in age and pace of change.
- growth leveling off for most and growing acceptance of own body.
- better able to manage strength and coordination.
- some resist commitments, wanting to be open to what future may bring.
- ethnic youths sometimes become personally concerned with cultural awareness.
- select peer groups become more important/consume majority of waking hours.

- some catch up physically with others. Sexual fantasies often evident with pressure for experimentation. Searching for sexual identification.
- establishing role models that may/may not go on in future.
- leadership roles become more evident and sometimes create conflicts.
- both same-sex and opposite-sex friendships, many one-on-one.
- some become "closer friends" to parents and some develop more conflict. This relationship often mellows in later years.
- adult to adult type relationships begin to develop with adults outside family, particularly in later years.
- some are reviewing established rules.
- some are inquiring into their faith, while others continue to accept specifics simply because they were "instructed" in it in the past.
- some find excitement in learning while others are bored.
- experience wide range of differences between 9th and 12th grades.
- school activities and sports often important.
- begin paying jobs which give them self-esteem but pressure them for time.
- most now drive and many have own cars, giving them more independence.
- some accept stereotypes, but many reject them.
- most can concentrate and enjoy longer times of idea exchanges.
- most are willing to try new ideas.
- some continue to seem flighty and unpredictable, but many take on responsibility and can manage difficult tasks.

The high schooler needs:
- many and varied active learning opportunities.
- opportunity to help shape their own activities and their own group direction.
- programs that are life centered, with biblical background.
- opportunity to engage directly/indirectly in worldwide ministry of church.
- adults who accept their ideas as valid and don't embarrass them.
- adults who affirm their own faith, encouraging them to think for themselves.
- adults who will "search" with them for answers.
- persons who will listen and accept their ideas as valid.
- adults who will help them develop their global understanding.
- opportunities to develop a sense of importance in the church.
- affirmation and recognition for accomplishment.
- opportunities to use their forming leadership abilities.

Parents of high schoolers need:
- to know just what's happening and when.
- to have regular opportunities for discussion with leaders.
- help in knowing how to prepare their high schooler for independent life.
- opportunity to be a part of the program.

---

1. Delia Halverson, *32 Ways to Become a Great Sunday School Teacher* (Nashville: Abingdon Press, 1997), pp. 17-23.

Young Reader's Bulletin

YOUNG READER'S BULLETIN

_____ Church
Hometown, USA

_____
(date)

Before the service begins:
1. Greet people around you before the prelude begins.
2. As the music begins, listen quietly and prepare for worship.
3. Locate the hymns in your hymnal and mark them.
4. Locate the scripture in the pew Bible and mark the place.
5. Fill in the name of someone or something you want to pray about during Morning Prayers.
6. Look for the asterisk (*) to know when we stand.
7. Give a smile of love to your parent(s).
8. Pray for those who lead us and that God helps us worship.

PRELUDE   (We prepare for worship. Listen to the organ and think of God's love.)

CONCERNS OF THE CHURCH
(Write or draw something mentioned to remember this week. Be sure to remind your parents that Wednesday night's pick-up time is now 7:15 P.M. sharp.)

MEDITATION AND SILENT CONFESSION
(Think of something you have done wrong that you want to change. Write or draw it here.)

RESPONSE TO GOD'S GIVING

*Doxology
   Praise God from whom all blessings flow.
   Praise him all creatures here below.
   Praise him above ye heavenly hosts.
   Praise Father, Son, and Holy Ghost. Amen.

Offertory (We give God some of what God has given us. As the organ plays, write or draw a special good thing that happened to you this week.)

SCRIPTURE   Matthew 28:16-20 Page 967
(Listen to and read the scripture. This is a special command that Jesus gave everyone who is to follow him. What does Jesus say we are to do? How does Jesus say he will help us to do this?)

MINISTRY OF MUSIC   Chancel Choir
(Listen to the words of the anthem and draw a picture that explains what the words say.)

CALL TO WORSHIP (from John 1)

Leader: In the beginning was the Word, and the Word was with God, and the word was God.
People: In Him Was Life and the Life Was the Light of All.
Leader: The light shines in the darkness and the darkness has not overcome it.
People: The True Light That Enlightens Everyone Was Coming into the World.

*HYMN 53 . . . . *Fairest Lord Jesus*

***PRAYER OF INVOCATION AND
OUR LORD'S PRAYER**

Our Father, who art in heaven, hallowed be thy name. Thy kingdom come, thy will be done on earth as it is in heaven. Give us this day our daily bread. And forgive us our trespasses, as we forgive those who trespass against us. And lead us not into temptation, but deliver us from evil. For thine is the kingdom, and the power, and the glory, forever. Amen.

*GLORIA PATRI

Glory be to the Father, and to the Son, and to the Holy Ghost.
As it was in the beginning, is now, and ever shall be.
World without end. Amen. Amen.

CHILDREN'S CHOIR

(Your time to lead the people in praising God.)

CHILDREN'S MOMENT (Join the pastor in the front.)

MORNING PRAYERS

PRELUDE TO PRAYER #438 . . . . *Seek Ye First*

Moment of Silent Prayer

(Remember persons for whom you specially want to pray. Write the names below.)

_____   _____

_____   _____

_____   _____

MESSAGE (The Pastor)

To Grow in Christ and to Make Christ Known

(Listen as the pastor explains what we pledge to do as a part of our church.
Write or draw something you can do to "grow in Christ" or to become a better Christian.)

*HYMN 497 . . . . *O Zion Haste*

*BENEDICTION

(The pastor sends us into the world to live as God wants us to live.)

*CONGREGATIONAL RESPONSE

In Christ there is no east or west,
in him no south or north;
but one great fellowship of love
throughout the whole wide earth.

CHOIR RECESSIONAL

ORGAN POSTLUDE (As you leave, remember that God is with you through the week.
Don't forget Sunday School at 10:15 A.M.)

Work Camp/ Mission Preplanning

Goals we hope will be accomplished with this event:

For participants: _____

_____

For recipients: _____

_____

Who will be involved? _____

Members of the planning committee? (include vision folks, detail folks, and persons with spiritual depth)

_____

_____

_____

What sort of experience is the group capable of? (heavy/light physical work, VBS leadership, construction,

medical/dental, etc.)_____

_____

If youth event, what adults might go along? What is their expertise?_____

_____

_____

Length of time for event? _____

Date possibilities _____

Where (with what agencies) might this take place?_____

_____

Transportation plans _____

_____

Prior to event:

• Group-building activities _____

_____

- Training activities _____

_____

- Dedication of mission (in service, just before leaving, etc.)_____

_____

In-church publicity _____

_____

Community publicity before/after (Remember that publicity about your mission spreads Christ and your
   church's mission to the community.)_____

_____

Event rules_____

_____

Equipment and supplies needed _____

_____

Lodging plans_____

_____

Meal plans_____

_____

_____

Spiritual enrichment plans _____

_____

Budget:_____

_____

_____

Additional plans:

Some ways to follow up/evaluate: _____

_____

_____

The Nuts & Bolts of Christian Education

Retreat Preplanning

A retreat is a time and place set apart from the ordinary events of life that encourages people to relate to one another through a variety of events centered on a common theme.

Who will be involved? _____

What do we hope will happen?_____

_____

Members of the planning committee?_____

_____

Possible counselors (if youth retreat)_____

_____

Curriculum/resources_____

Group-building activities _____

_____

Other activities_____

_____

Amount of time   ☐ one day   ☐ overnight   ☐ weekend

Date preference _____   Alternative dates _____

Transportation plans _____

_____

Child care _____

Publicity plans _____

_____

_____

Meals ☐ cook in ☐ catered ☐ eat out ☐ each provide own

Food possibilities _____

_____

Possible schedule—include worship, study, play, meals, lights out, and/or free time

_____   _____

_____   _____

_____   _____

_____   _____

_____   _____

_____   _____

_____   _____

Retreat rules _____

_____

_____

Facility requirements ☐ cabin/bunks ☐ private rooms ☐ meeting room (size ____) ☐ dining with others

 ☐ dining in private group ☐ chapel ☐ outdoor facility requirements_____

 ☐ child-care facility ☐ other _____

Facility possibilities _____

Budget

Additional notes _____

Some ways to follow up/evaluate _____

Field Trip Planning Worksheet

Trip Name _____ Date _____

Theme and Purpose _____

_____

_____

Scripture _____

Time: Pre-trip _____

      Travel _____

      On-site _____

      Debrief _____

      Other _____

      Total _____

On-site Contact Person _____ Phone _____

Address _____ Zip _____

Location/directions _____

_____

_____

Approximate # expected _____ Pre-registered #_____ Final # _____

Cost: Total _____ Per person _____ ☐ Paid (date) _____

Pre-trip study plans _____

Follow-up study plans _____

Meal/refreshments plan _____

_____

Publicity plan _____

_____

☐ Letter written to on-site contact confirming details (date) _____

☐ Letter/call for final confirmation and number just prior to event

☐ Letter of thanks written after trip

☐ Pre-registration forms sent (deadline _____)

☐ Permission slips prepared (Include emergency phone numbers, permission for emergency medical treatment, and notary signature.)

☐ Drivers: _____

☐ Instructions for drivers: Map/directions, phone number, rules (see below), rider names (pre-assigned); schedule, taking a head-count

☐ Name tags for participants

☐ Establish and print rules to be read aloud before EACH field trip. (Use low voices so everyone can hear the guide; do not run; stay with the group; wear your seat belts; respect the driver.)

Additional Notes:

Hanging of the Greens

(Sunday Morning Worship)

Here's a new twist for Sunday morning. It takes very little time during the corporate worship because you weave it into your regular order of worship, and people of all ages have an opportunity to participate. Here's how one church set it up. Adjust it according to your usual litany of worship.

After the Prelude
    Leader: The prophet Isaiah wrote, "Prepare the way of the Lord." Let us prepare our worship area as we prepare our hearts for the coming of Christ. (*Dim the lights.*)

After Introit (*with lights dimmed*)
    Leader: The world sat in darkness, waiting for the light.
    All: **Our Lord, we await your coming. We recognize our need for your forgiveness and your love.**

    (*Brief silence for personal reflection.*)
    Choir: "Morning Has Broken." (*As the choir sings, the tree lights are lit.*)

Processional Hymn "Joyful, Joyful, We Adore Thee"

Call to Worship (*During this reading garlands are brought up the aisles and hung as planned.*)
    Leader: God placed vegetation on the earth to sustain us and to renew the earth. Our plants give us food and shelter, and through their humus the soil is renewed.
    All: **Thank you, God, for your plan for renewed life.**
         Thank you for Christ who gives us new life.
    Leader: As the green plants take in carbon dioxide and give off oxygen, the air on which we depend is renewed.
    All: **We come to this Advent season anticipating the renewal of your covenant through Christ.**
    Leader: As the evergreen tree is forever green, so we know that we can depend on God's love forever. We also know that through Christ's life we can experience life eternal.
    All: **As you give us eternal life, we pledge our constant love and service to you.**

Placement of Wreaths (*After reading, special music or a hymn may be sung as wreaths are completed.*)
    Leader: The circle of the wreaths has no beginning and no end, just as God's love has no beginning and no end. The red bows represent the ultimate sacrifice, when Jesus gave his life for us.

Lighting Advent Candle

Children's Moment (*Invite children to come to the front for Advent Affirmation of Faith and explanations of the Chrismons. The Chrismons are placed on tree during the reading and anthem.*)

Advent Affirmation of Faith
- **All:** We believe in the one true God, almighty and greater than any king clothed in purple and gold.
- **Leader:** In the ancient world, purple was a scarce color and therefore used by royalty. The color of Advent is purple, reminding us of the royalty of Christ. The crown reminds us that Jesus Christ is king of our lives.
- **All:** We believe that God came to us in human form, as Messiah and Savior of all the world.
- **Leader:** The shepherd's crook reminds us of those shepherds who first visited the Christ Child, and it reminds us that Jesus told stories of how God cares for us as a shepherd. The star reminds us of the night when angels sang and a brilliant star marked the birth of Jesus, our promised Messiah.
- **All:** We believe in God, revealed in three ways but truly one.
- **Leader:** The Greek letters on our tree represent various names for Jesus: Christ, Savior, Son of God. The first and last letters of the Greek alphabet, alpha and omega, remind us that Christ is with us from the beginning to the end.
- **All:** We believe that Christ died for us so that we might live forever.
- **Leader:** The various crosses remind us of that death.
- **All:** We believe that Christ sent a Comforter to be with us, even after his death.
- **Leader:** Jesus told us to be fishers of people. The fish represents Christians who kept their faith during the times of persecution. They used the fish as a secret symbol so that we might know about Christ today.
- **All:** We believe that Christ calls us to follow him today.

Gloria Patri
Anthem
Scripture Reading and Prayers

Placing of Crèche
- **Leader:** The villagers of Greccio, Italy, in 1223, stood in awe as a dark, dismal cave came to life with the Christmas story. Saint Francis of Assisi envisioned this method of telling the story of Christ's birth with a live manger scene, complete with animals. Today we use the crèche to remind us that the story is real.
- **All:** Thank you, God, for coming in human form. Through Christ we understand you better.
- **Leader:** Although the shepherds and wise men came at different times, we include them both in our manger scene. This reminds us that Christ came for all of us, no matter what our circumstances.

Hymn "Away in a Manger"

Receiving of Tithes and Offerings
- **Leader:** As Christ comes to each of us, we must share Christ with others. Through our gifts and talents we share Christ.

(For the remainder of the service follow the usual form. Any additional decorations may be added during the next week.)

1. Originally published in *Leader in the Church School Today* (summer 2000).

Planning Checklist

Name of Event _____ Date(s)_____ Time_____

☐ On church calendar?

Purpose_____

_____

Participants (age, interest, etc.) _____

_____

Location, rooms, etc._____

☐ Room reservation requested. Must be done by _____.

Room setup:_____

☐ Setup given to custodian. Must be done by _____.

Resources/Curriculum_____

☐ Ordered? Date _____

Child care? ☐ Arrangements made   ☐ Must be arranged for by_____

Refreshments? _____ Person responsible _____

Leader/teacher/director _____ Phone _____

Outline/plan:

Publicity plan

Accomplished	Date due in office	Date(s) of announcement	Person responsible
☐ Newsletter	_____	_____	_____
☐ Bulletin	_____	_____	_____
☐ Local newspaper	_____	_____	_____
☐ Posters	_____	_____	_____
☐ Mailing	_____	_____	_____

To whom? _____

Approximate # expected _____ Preregistered # _____ Final #_____

Cost/budget _____ per person _____

Education Committee Budget

	Last Year	Next Year
A. Curriculum		
Children, Youth, Adults	$ _____	$ _____

Comments about changes:

B. Supplies   _____   _____

Comments about changes:

C. Confirmation/Graduate Gifts   _____   _____

Comments about changes:

D. Leadership Development/Recognition   _____   _____

(Schools, Workshops: registration fees, transportation, lodging,

food, honorarium, supplies.

Appreciation: events, gifts, letters, etc.)

Comments about changes:

	Last Year	Next Year
E. Library/Resource Center	_____	_____
Comments about changes:		
F. Child Care	_____	_____
Comments about changes:		
G. Youth Choir Music/Supplies	_____	_____
Comments about changes:		
H. Vacation Bible School	_____	_____
Comments about changes:		
I. Classroom Equipment & Repair	_____	_____
Comments about changes:		
J. Miscellaneous	_____	_____
Comments about changes:		
Totals	_____	_____

Additional comments:

Evaluations

A Sandwich Evaluation

When we balance our recommendations with commendations, we make our evaluations more tasteful. With a balanced diet, we grow in our ministry to Christ and the church.

In the sandwich below, begin with the bottom slice of bread and write words or short statements about your class in the corresponding categories.

7. **Olive** — Top it off with at least one area to improve in the next session.

6. **Bread** — Another commendation, holding the evaluation together.

5. **Pickles** — When we had a pickle of a problem.

4. **Lettuce** — Let us rejoice over a particularly good experience.

3. **Meat** — Some recommendations for change.

2. **Cheese** — What are some concerns of a student that were apparent in the session?

1. **Bread** — Evaluations need to begin with commendations. What was good?

It is important that the steps be in the order indicated above. This mixes the good comments with the not so good ones—and tops the session off with a firm decision for improvement.

1. Delia Halverson, *How to Train Volunteer Teachers* (Nashville: Abingdon Press, 1991).

Children's Council Review

In Our Church

We currently meet these needs:

Program/Event:	What need met and how:
_____	_____
_____	_____
_____	_____
_____	_____

We can improve this program/event:

By doing this:

_____   _____

_____   _____

_____   _____

_____   _____

We can meet these additional needs:

With this:

_____   _____

_____   _____

_____   _____

_____   _____

Ways we can involve children in leadership and planning of their own programs:

_____   _____

_____   _____

_____   _____

Family Registration for Summer Activities and Fall Sunday School

Family name _____

Address _____ Zip _____ Phone _____

Parent name(s) _____

Address of a parent if different from child _____ Phone _____

Location of parent at   8:30 A.M. _____   9:45 A.M. _____   11:00 A.M. _____

Child #1:

Last name _____   First name _____   Name used _____

Date of birth: Month _____   Day _____   Year _____   Grade Sept. 2001 _____

Any health or allergy alerts _____

Grade of school completed in spring _____   Classroom assignment _____ (to be filled in by office)

Child #2:

Last name _____   First name _____   Name used _____

Date of birth: Month _____   Day _____   Year _____   Grade Sept. 2001 _____

Any health or allergy alerts _____

Grade of school completed in spring _____   Classroom assignment _____ (to be filled in by office)

Child #3:

Last name _____   First name _____   Name used _____

Date of birth: Month _____   Day _____   Year _____   Grade Sept. 2001 _____

Any health or allergy alerts _____

Grade of school completed in spring _____   Classroom assignment _____ (to be filled in by office)

These are:

_____ continuing students   _____ new students   ____ visitors   ____ one time visitors only

I would also like to register my children for the following summer activities:

Vacation Bible School (date)   Children's names: _____

_____ (date)   Children's names: _____

_____ (date)   Children's names: _____

_____ (date)   Children's names: _____

Amount attached: _____   (if fee is required for activities)

Emergency/ Fire Escape Plan

Every church needs an emergency plan, whether for fire or natural disaster. Work with this form to begin planning yours. Work with a committee representing persons who use all areas of the building. After approval, post the plan at conspicuous places and inform all teachers, ushers, and so forth. Set aside a time to test the plan when there is no emergency.

List below ideas for established rules for leaving (such as shut off heaters, close doors behind you, alert other classes along route, extinguish flames on fire victims with rug or by rolling on floor, prearranged place to gather outside building after leaving, signal for reentering building, and so forth).

_____

_____

_____

Consider these questions:

- The workers in classrooms with small children cannot evacuate all of the children alone.

  What adult classes can get to the nursery easily to help?_____

  _____

  What adult classes will be assigned to which classroom of small children? _____

  _____

- During worship, who will be responsible for assisting nursery workers? _____

  _____

- What sort of fire alarms do you have? Can they be heard everywhere? _____

- Are smoke detectors installed at appropriate places? _____ Where do you need additional detectors?

  _____

- Consider using a rope with knots tied every 2 feet in the preschool classrooms. Children learn to hold on to the knot while walking down the hall in a line. This practice prepares them for orderly exits. Plan a convenient place for the rope near the door but out of children's reach.

- How will the plan be altered to adjust for natural disasters? _____

- List suggestions for fire prevention procedures in your church (such as learning number for fire department, fire extinguishers serviced yearly, policy on use of candles, and so forth).

Duplicate the floorplan of each building. Map out and mark primary and alternate routes for each room and post the plan just inside the door.

Sample Permission Slip

NOTE: Check with your local legal advisors before finalizing any permission slips. Your insurance or local regulations may determine the wording.

Sample Permission Slips

   I hereby give permission for _____ to accompany his/her class/group and staff persons on _____ field trip/retreat as planned by _____ Church. It is my understanding that only authorized vehicles and drivers will be used.

   I understand that the church/weekday program has insurance coverage which includes this trip.

   I also give permission for my child to be included in any pictures in connection with this program.

Date _____ Signed _____

Child's name (please print) _____

Parent or legal guardian's name (please print) _____

Phone number for contact _____

Alternate phone contact: Name _____ Number _____

Date _____ Signed _____
(parent or legal guardian)

- -

Emergency Treatment

In the event of an illness or accident that requires immediate medical treatment to_____ at a time when a parent cannot be located, I give permission for an approved representative of _____ Church to authorize such treatment. I will not hold the church or medical personnel responsible. In signing this I understand that every attempt will be made to contact the child/youth's parents/ legal guardian, physician, or other persons listed for emergency contact.

Date _____ Signed _____
(parent or legal guardian)

Physician _____ Phone _____

Other persons who may be notified if parents/legal guardian cannot be contacted:

Name   Phone

_____   _____

_____   _____

_____   _____

Guidelines for Selecting Bible Stories

As we consider specific stories for certain age groups, we need to recognize the levels of perception and skill of the children and youth. One of the primary factors to consider is the ability to think abstractly. When our son was five, one of his friends asked, "What is the word that is something like a million?" Another friend said, "You mean a dozen?" The first responded with excitement, "Yeah, there were a dozen of them!" Young children bring this same sort of understanding to the story of Jesus feeding the multitude. They can, however, appreciate the fact that Jesus cared when the people were hungry, and that there was a boy in the crowd who shared.

In all miracle stories shared with young children, we need to emphasize the caring aspect of Jesus. We certainly want to help both children and youth realize that miracles are different from magic. Magic is built on illusions.

Next, let's look at the stories themselves. We need not feel that a child or a youth must be familiar with every story in the Bible, but there are basic stories that we hope they will know by the time they reach adulthood.

Your church may have a curriculum goal that includes a specific list of stories. If not, consider the list below. Of course, each child is different, and you need to seriously consider each situation. If a story is introduced when it relates to a current life experience, then the story has more meaning.

Specific Ages to Introduce Suggested Stories

Younger Preschool

Old Testament
God Made the World (Genesis 1:1, 27, 31)

New Testament
Birth of Jesus (Luke 2:1-7)
Shepherds Hear the Good News (Luke 2:8-20)
Jesus Grew and Helped Joseph (Luke 2:39-40)
A Boy Shares His Lunch of Loaves and Fishes (John 6:1-14)
Jesus Helps Jairus' Daughter (Luke 8:40-42, 49-56)

(New Testament cont.)
Zacchaeus (Luke 19:1-10)
Jesus Loves the Children (Luke 18:15-17)
Jesus Rides into Jerusalem (Mark 11:1-11)
Jesus' Last Supper (Matthew 26:17-20, 26-28; Mark 14:17-25; Luke 22:14-20)
Jesus' Enemies Killed Him, but God Didn't Let Jesus Stay Dead (treated together in simple form—Matthew 27:35*a*, 57-60; 28:1-8)
Jesus Has a Cookout with His Friends (omitting when it happened—John 21:1-13)

Older Preschool

Old Testament

The Big Flood (Genesis 6:14, 19-22, 7:17, 8:1-20, 9:13-15)

(Do not emphasize the sinfulness of the world here. Older preschoolers' abstract thinking is not advanced enough.)

Abraham's Faithful Journey (Genesis 12:1-5)

Miriam Cares for Her Brother (Exodus 2:1-10)

Ruth Is Kind to Her Mother-in-Law (Ruth 2)

Samuel Helps Eli (1 Samuel 2:18)

Solomon Builds the Temple (1 Kings 5–8, selected)

New Testament

Mary's Promise of a Child (Luke 1:26-38) (Ignore the virginity of Mary. Older preschoolers are too young to understand.)

Visit of the Wise Men (Matthew 2:1-2, 9-11)

Presentation of Baby Jesus at the Temple (Luke 2:22-39)

Jesus Teaches in the Synagogue (Luke 4:14-30)

Jesus Calms the Storm (Mark 4:35-41)

Jesus' Story of the Lost Sheep (Luke 15:3-7)

One of Ten Tells Jesus Thank You (Luke 17:11-19)

The Birthday of the Church (Acts 1:4-5, 13-14, 2:1-17, 22-47)

Younger Elementary

Old Testament

Creation (Genesis 1:1–2:3)

Tower of Babel (Genesis 11:1-9)

Isaac Is Born (Genesis 21:1-7)

Moses and the Wanderings (Exodus 1–20, selected)

Battle of Jericho (Joshua 6:1-20)

God Calls Samuel (1 Samuel 3:1-10, 19-20)

David and Goliath (1 Samuel 17:1-58)

David and Jonathan (1 Samuel 19–20, selected)

A Woman and Her Son Care for Elijah (1 Kings 17:8-15)

The Boy, Jeremiah, Answers God (Jeremiah 1:4-8)

New Testament

Escape with Baby Jesus to Egypt (Matthew 2:13-23)

Jesus as a Boy in the Temple (Luke 2:41-52)

John the Baptist Tells of Jesus' Coming (Matthew 3:1-12)

Jesus' Baptism (Matthew 3:13-17)

Jesus' Temptation (Luke 4:1-15)

Jesus Invites Friends to Follow Him (Luke 5:1-11; Matthew 9:35–10:8)

(New Testament cont.)

Jesus Attends a Wedding (John 2:1-12)

Friends Bring to Jesus a Man Who Cannot Walk (Mark 2:1-12)

Jesus Heals a Lame Man at the Pool (John 5:1-15)

Parable of Good Samaritan (Luke 10:25-37)

Jesus' Friends, Mary and Martha (Luke 10:38-42)

Jesus Teaches About Prayer (Luke 11:1-4; Matthew 6:7-15)

Parable of the Forgiving Father (Luke 15:11-32)

Jesus Heals a Deaf Man (Mark 7:31-37)

Jesus and the Moneychangers (John 2:13-22)

The Resurrection (Matthew 28:1-10; Luke 24:1-12; John 20:1-18)

Philip Tells of Jesus (Acts 8:26-40)

The Road to Damascus (Acts 9:1-25)

Lydia, the Businesswoman (Acts 16:11-15)

An Earthquake at the Jail (Acts 16:16-40)

Older Elementary

Old Testament
- The Garden of Eden (Genesis 3)
- God's Covenant with Noah (Genesis 6:5–9:17)
- Esau and Jacob (Genesis 25:20-34, 32:3-21; 33:1-4)
- Joseph (Genesis 37–47)
- Deborah, the Judge and Prophetess (Judges 4:4-23)
- Ruth and Naomi (Ruth)
- King David (1 and 2 Samuel, selected)
- Elijah and the Prophets of Baal (1 Kings 18:1, 17-45)
- Queen Esther (Esther)
- Daniel in the Lions' Den (Daniel 6)
- Jonah Runs from God (Jonah)

New Testament
- Birth of John the Baptist (Luke 1:5-25, 57-80)
- Disciples Pick Grain on the Sabbath (Mark 2:23-28)

(New Testament cont.):
- Parable of the Sower (Matthew 13:1-9, 18-23)
- Jesus Walks on Water (Matthew 14:22-33)
- Two Men Praying in the Temple (Luke 18:9-14)
- Lazarus (John 11:1-44)
- Parable of Servants' Use of Money (Matthew 25:14-30)
- A Woman Who Washed Jesus' Feet (Luke 7:36-50)
- Last Supper, Gethsemane, Trial, Crucifixion (Matthew 26:14–27:66)
- Thomas Finally Believes (John 20:19-29)
- Friends Traveling to Emmaus (Luke 24:13-35)
- Stephen, the First Christian Martyr (Acts 6:8–8:1)
- Peter Escapes from Jail (Acts 12:1-19)
- Paul's Missionary Journeys (Acts 13–28)

Middle School

Old Testament
- Two Creation Stories (Genesis 1:1–2:25)
- God's Covenant with Abraham (Genesis 12–15)
- Abraham Obeys God (Genesis 22:1-19) (Note: "Obeys" is more affirmative than Abraham's "testing.")
- Babylonian Exile (2 Chronicles, selected)
- Valley of Dry Bones (Ezekiel 37:1-14)

New Testament:
- Kingdom of God Is Like a Mustard Seed (Mark 4:30-34)
- Jesus Sends His Followers Out to Teach (Luke 10:1-12, 16-20)

(New Testament cont.)
- Parable of the Unmerciful Servant (Matthew 18:23-35)
- Parable of Workers in the Vineyard (Matthew 20:1-16)
- Parable of Two Sons (Matthew 21:28-31)
- Parable of Invitations to a Wedding (Matthew 22:1-10; Luke 14:15-24)
- Transfiguration of Jesus (Luke 9:28-36)
- The Widow's Gift (Mark 12:41-44)
- I Was Hungry and You Fed Me (Matthew 25:31-46)
- Jesus Taken Up into Heaven (Acts 1:1-11)
- Peter Heals a Man (Acts 3:1-10)

High School

Old Testament
- Rahab's Story (Joshua 2:1-24, 6:1-25)
- Abigail Helps David (1 Samuel 25, 27:2-3, 30:1-6, 18)
- Elijah and the Chariots of Fire (2 Kings 2:1-15)
- A Good Man Has Problems (Job)

New Testament
- Jesus Tells of a Dinner Party (Luke 14:1, 7-14)
- Parable of the Persistent Widow (Luke 18:1-8)
- Parable of Ten Women with Lamps (Matthew 25:1-13)
- Jesus' Death (Luke 23:26-47)
- The Holy City (Revelation 21)

Agenda

Committee: _____

Meeting Agenda

Date _____

AGENDA	*ACTION/NOTES*
Praise and Singing	
Telling the Story (Where do you see God working in self/church?)	
Offering (items to be planned, reviewed)	
Sending forth (How/when will we carry out our offering to God?)	

Copies to: _____

Plan
of
Action

Date _____   Project Name _____

Description _____

_____

_____

Purpose/Goal(s)_____

_____

Target(s)   Deadline

☐ _____   _____

☐ _____   _____

☐ _____   _____

☐ _____   _____

Person(s) Involved   Phone   Responsibility

_____   _____   _____

_____   _____   _____

_____   _____   _____

_____   _____   _____

_____   _____   _____

_____   _____   _____

The Nuts & Bolts of Christian Education

Mother's Morning In

Stay-at-home moms today are sometimes the only adults at home in a five-block radius, and they often feel that they can't visit other stay-at-home moms without calling ahead and making an appointment. A Mother's Morning In is how we met this need 15 years ago when I worked at Roswell United Methodist Church in Roswell, Georgia. This gathering was informal enough that mothers weren't encumbered with organizational requirements and yet had easy opportunity for adult fellowship. The group still meets.

Mother's Morning In met twice a month, and it was organized for MOTHERS, not the children. The object was to offer stay-at-home moms a support group and opportunity for some challenging study. It also became a great doorway for young couples to come into the church family. Mothers who belonged told neighbors and friends about it and felt comfortable in inviting them, since it was not Bible oriented or overly "religious." Later, after the nonmember mothers became acquainted, they easily moved into a young adult Sunday school class. We did have child care, and for that we hired retired grandparents. The church subsidized the cost, so the mother was charged only $1.00 per child.

The group first met three weeks in a row and got acquainted with each other. They also decided just what they wanted the program to include. Their decision was that they would meet two Tuesdays a month (our United Methodist Women met on one Tuesday) and the programs would be on parenting skills, self-improvement, or spousal relations. We began to gather at 9:30. During the first half hour mothers settled their children in the nursery and visited over coffee and tea. They took turns bringing some sort of goodies. Then at 10:00 we began our meeting, handling any "business" quickly and moving on to cares and concerns and then to our program. We were through between 11:00 and 11:15, as some had to pick up children at preschool by 11:30.

Our meeting programs varied. For one meeting the city librarian spoke about how to involve young children in reading, and we brought some kids from the nursery for her to read to and illustrate this. Another time we discussed how they could use their volunteer work as some reference on resumes that they might write later if they wanted to go back to work. One week everyone brought healthy snacks and the recipes, and we even made up a little booklet for the recipes.

One of the greatest pluses was a list that we passed around periodically. It included places to sign if you had had particular situations, such as a child in the hospital, a child with temper tantrums, a death in the family, or other concerns. If you put your name and phone number on the list, then anyone could call you for support if they found themselves in a similar situation.

There was such a need for this support group, and it was so well received that we averaged sixty mothers. Everyone knew they could come when they liked; but if they had an occasion that kept them away even at the last minute, they just didn't show up. Finally, we developed neighborhood groups within the group, and those in each neighborhood group chose to get together once a month in some configuration. Some groups went to the playground with their children. Some selected an evening to go out to dinner and leave their children with the fathers. But it gave them another opportunity to get together with a smaller group.

Children's Coordinator

(Sample Job Description)

PRIMARY TASK

Lead the Children's Council in searching for special concerns that children have today and in exploring possibilities of enhancing relationships, study, service, and worship with and for children in the church.

Children's Council is optional and may be organized with regular meetings or an informal group of persons who are interested in children and what happens to them. It would be good for the Council to include persons responsible for coordinating regular programs in the church such as weekday programs, kindergarten, children's choir, nursery, and so forth.

BASIC RESPONSIBILITIES (suggested—each church will vary):
— Be aware of the needs of the children in the church and community.
— Look at programs already in existence that may meet these needs.
— Educate the congregation about the needs of children.
— Work with directors of any ongoing programs for children in the church.
— Be aware of condition of facilities used by children and pass on to the trustees any suggestions for their improvement.
— See that all child care and programming for children is coordinated and well planned and supervised.

SUGGESTED SCHEDULE

(adjusted according to local needs)

Jan. Set date for and recruit director of vacation Bible school and other summer programs.

Evaluate programs in relation to needs of children.

Recruit workers for Lenten activities for children.

Feb. Check on Lenten plans for children.

*Mar. Be sure summer activities are publicized and leaders are being recruited. (Include conference camping opportunities.)

Apr. Consult with director(s) of weekday program(s) for any way that you can assist with plans for next year and preregistration.

If preregistration for summer activities is used, make final plans.

If preregistration for fall classes is used, make final plans.

May Plan for fall Bible presentation and see that Bibles are ordered.

Preregistration for summer activities.

Preregistration for fall classes.

June–July Check on progress of summer activities.

Provide additional opportunity for fall class registration.

Aug. Mail letters to parents of children to receive Bibles and plan presentation.

Sept. Plan for Advent activities and recruit director(s).

Oct. Recruit workers for Advent activities.

Nov.–Dec. Finalize and carry out Advent activities.

Plan Lenten activities and recruit director.

*Note: In some churches, the Children's Coordinator may be responsible for recruiting children's teachers. If so, begin fall recruitment in March.

Mission (Job) Description

Sunday School Teacher
from
St. Luke's United Methodist Church
Orlando, Florida — 1993

WHAT IS THE TASK?

With the aid of a coteacher(s), you will

1. plan lessons designed to share the good news of Christ's love and meet the age-level and special needs of your class members.
2. pray for your class members.
3. invite visitors to your class and encourage the class members to do the same.
4. attend worship services regularly and encourage class members to do same.
5. be in attendance at Sunday school as often as possible (every week is ideal, but of course, not always possible).
6. arrive in your classroom by 9:15 or 10:45 A.M. if at all possible.
7. when appropriate, make contact outside of classroom with students, birthday cards, "we miss you" cards, phone calls, and so forth.

TRAINING OFFERED

Please attend at least one of the following:

1. Our own training event will be held Saturday morning _____

2. Conference Sunday School Weekend _____

3. Teachers' Meeting/Training "Spots" _____

TIME COMMITMENT INVOLVED

Pick one option:

_____ 12 month commitment, _____ to _____

_____ 9 month commitment, _____ to _____

_____ Summer commitment, _____ to _____

Sundays: 9:15-10:45 or 10:45-12:15 and weekly preparation of about 2 hours

Weekly total—about 3.5 hours. Monthly total—about 13 hours.

Quarterly teachers meetings—1.5 hours once every three months (summer excluded).

YOU WILL RECEIVE

1. Curriculum resources spelling out the weekly lesson plan.
2. Training for the task.
3. Support through quarterly written "How To" help—a subscription.
4. Support through supplies and other resources made available for you.
5. Moral and prayerful support from the Sunday school leadership and pastors.
6. Child care available for the quarterly meetings and training events.
7. A feeling of contributing to the kingdom of God through the education of God's people and being a part of the work of ministry.
8. A sense of being a part of something extremely significant in the lives of your students.

Sample Mission Description

Director of Christian Education

Summary statement of responsibilities:

To work primarily with the Pastor and the Education Committee to develop and supervise the Christian Education Ministry within our church and as it reaches out to others.

QUALIFICATIONS:

Sincere commitment to Christ and his church

Teaching and leadership experience

Christian Education degree or comparable education and experience or dedication to taking such training

Ability to relate to and work with all ages

Ability to teach and lead adults, youth, and children

Ability to recognize leadership potential in others and to nurture it

Strong interpersonal and organizational skills

ACCOUNTABILITY:

To the Pastor as immediate supervisor, ultimately to the church governing body through the Education Committee.

DUTIES:

1. Train, resource and support the entire Christian Education team.

   a. Be available for teachers and leaders by appointment.

   b. Keep abreast of new resources.

   c. See that appropriate curriculum is ordered.

   d. Coordinate workshops and training seminars.

   e. Serve as resource person for all teachers and leaders.

   f. Encourage support of the Christian Education team through letters, phone calls, and planned appreciation events.

2. Serve on Sunday school and other educational program committees, as an advisory member of the Education Committee, and as an ex officio member of church program committee and governing board.

3. Assist the Education Committee in assessing Christian Education needs and setting long and short-range goals.

4. Work toward implementation of new Christian Education programs to carry out set goals.

5. See that Christian Education programs are promoted in traditional and creative ways.

6. Work with other church groups and committees, assisting them as they use educational methods and helping to coordinate Christian Education programs and ideas with other programs and activities.

7. Participate in a wide variety of church functions and activities to foster positive relationships within the church family and to become acquainted with persons, thereby helping persons find their place of ministry within the church. This will include new member meetings where possible.

8. Cooperate with the pastor and the Worship Committee to share some regular responsibility for children's sermons, announcements, scriptures, and so forth in order to have exposure to the congregation.

9. Cooperate with the Worship Committee on worship nursery, seeing that volunteers (huggers) are available to assist the paid worker.

10. Oversee Library/Resource Center to include coordinating and supporting volunteers, recommending purchases, maintaining materials and equipment.

11. Supervise educational equipment, supplies and materials.

12. Maintain financial accounts for all Christian Education programs.

13. Maintain program files for all Christian Education programs, assisting volunteer leaders with evaluations and summary reports.

14. Attend all staff meetings.

15. Perform other tasks as agreed upon with pastor.

16. Prepare annually a list of personal goals to be used in evaluation interviews.

17. Organize your time so as to provide opportunity for personal spiritual enrichment, vocational development, and family time.

Reflections for Teachers

The questions below will help you reflect on some of your beliefs and how you will approach students. There are no right or wrong answers. Use additional paper if you want, and express your thoughts as fully as possible.

What is your reaction when someone disagrees with you about a belief? _____

_____

What significance does prayer have in your own life and why do you pray? _____

_____

What is the primary task of a Christian? _____

_____

What is your interpretation of these two statements of Jesus and how do they fit together?

"No one comes to the Father except through me."   (John 14:6*b*)

"Not everyone who says to me, 'Lord, Lord,' will enter the kingdom of heaven, but only the one who does the will of my Father in heaven."   (Matthew 7:21)

_____

_____

Do you believe the Bible to be without error? Why or why not? _____

_____

How does the Holy Spirit inspire us today as we read the Bible? _____

_____

Are there writers today who are inspired by God? _____

Which writers have you read lately? _____

_____

How would the Bible be different if it were written today? _____

_____

How does the Bible record our quest to understand God? _____

_____

How do you see God calling our church to be involved in today's world? _____

_____

In what ways do you see the church teaching Christianity? _____

_____

How does Christian education relate to other areas in the church? _____

_____

What is the relationship of the church to the problems we face today? _____

_____

How do you hope your students will be able to profess their faith? _____

_____

Proposed Plan for Teacher Training

_____ Church

Work with this form for planning your training. In the left-hand column note which of the following categories each of the workshops falls under. Try to plan at least one in each category each year.

How to Train Volunteer Teachers.

1. Orientation and interpretation
   (information, goals, faith, and so forth)

2. Support
   (group building, get acquainted, and so forth)

3. Spiritual growth
   (Bible study, prayer, stewardship, and so forth)

4. Teaching method
   (storytelling, puppets, music, and so forth)

Consider your teachers. In what areas do you recognize specific needs? In what areas have you heard requests?

_____   _____

_____   _____

_____   _____

_____   _____

Special event training we will consider

Type of training	Whom targeted?	Resource and/or leader	Date	Est. Cost

District and regional training events we will encourage:

Dates   Event   Whom will we invite to attend?

_____

_____

_____

Regular interval training we will consider
Consider the routine schedule of your church and family responsibilities of your teachers. When are possible times to have regular training events? Consider times when they are already at the church building.

_____   _____

_____   _____

_____   _____

_____   _____

Type of interval training	Whom targeted?	Resource and/or leader	Date	Est. Cost

Experienced teachers: "Master Teachers" for in-classroom training.

_____   _____

_____   _____

_____   _____

_____   _____

Persons who will benefit from one-on-one training.

Person   Area of instruction needed

_____   _____

_____   _____

_____   _____

_____   _____

Will we consider a self-directed study?
See *32 Ways to Become a Great Sunday School Teacher* by Delia Halverson (Nashville: Abingdon Press, 1997).

Persons who will benefit from a self-directed study:

_____   _____

_____   _____

_____   _____

_____   _____

Teacher Training/Recognition Calendar

Sept.	Oct.	Nov.	Dec.
Jan.	Feb.	Mar.	Apr.
May	June	July	Aug.

Additional help can be found in *How to Train Volunteer Teachers*, chapter 4, by Delia Halverson (see Resources and References).

APPENDIX 23

Plan for Teacher Newsletter

Newsletters should contain information of interest to the teachers, but they should not be filled with "busy material" because we respect the teacher's time. Plan ample "white" space so that newsletters do not appear cluttered. Routine columns/articles need to be located at a regular place each time for quick recognition. Clip art adds to the newsletter but needs to be clear and related to the subject.

Person(s) on teaching staff or education committee who may be interested in editing newsletter:

_____   _____

_____   _____

_____   _____

Plan for printing _____

_____

_____

Frequency of newsletter: _____

_____

How will it be delivered?

☐ passed out before class

☐ left in class mail box at church

☐ mailed first class

Items to include in newsletter	Frequency	
	Regular	Occasional
Names/phone number of teaching staff	_____	_____
Names/phone number of substitutes	_____	_____
Upcoming teacher events	_____	_____
News of new equipment, supplies, and so forth	_____	_____
Teaching methods article	_____	_____
Inspirational/enrichment article	_____	_____
"It Worked for Me" article	_____	_____
Interview of a teacher	_____	_____
Joys and concerns of teaching staff	_____	_____
Seasonal items	_____	_____
"It was heard in class" (Tidbits from classrooms.)	_____	_____
_____	_____	_____
_____	_____	_____
_____	_____	_____
_____	_____	_____

Teacher's Handbook Plan

Handbook to be for teachers of ☐ all ages ☐ children ☐ youth ☐ adults

Handbook will be ☐ stapled ☐ in loose leaf binder ☐ spiral bound ☐ in folder

Handbook will be ☐ returned for reuse after teaching term ☐ kept indefinitely

When/how handbook will be given to teachers _____

Who will collect materials? _____

Who will review materials? _____

Plan for printing handbook _____

Possible items to be included. (Fill in blank with specifics from your church.)

☐ Objects, aims, or goals of Christian education.

☐ Curriculum information.

☐ Characteristics and understandings of age levels.

  (See appendix 1 "Adult Generations" and appendix 2 "Characteristics of Children and Youth")

☐ List of resources available in local church or at other levels. _____

_____

_____

_____

_____

☐ Procedures such as those for library, supply room, what to do with old curriculum, teachers' mail boxes, storage, and kitchen use. _____

_____

_____

☐ Class times, bells, offering procedure, registration, parties, custodial requirements/forms, and so forth.

_____

_____

☐ Calendar of training events, Sunday school events, and other church functions that are relevant to teachers.

_____

_____

☐ List of names and phone numbers of teachers, substitutes, staff, and denominational resource persons.

_____

_____

☐ Additional printed helps for teachers, such as reviews of books available in the library and copies of magazine articles (be sure to write for permission to reproduce).

_____

_____

_____

_____

The Sacrament of Baptism

> *Purpose:* **To help parents and children better understand the meaning of baptism.**

Sacrament

The word *sacrament* means literally "sacred moment," a time when humans come in contact with the divine. We observe two sacraments, baptism and Communion, which Jesus commanded us to observe. These events help us to taste, touch, feel, know, and experience the grace (or special love) of God. This grace is an unqualified, undeserved love. We receive grace without earning it. God's love says that even when at times we do not act in the way that God wants us to, God's love is there. Sometimes God loves with a happy heart, and sometimes God loves with a sad heart. But God always loves. We experience that love in the sacraments.

Preparation

- Ask families to bring reminders of their own baptism or any baptism they have seen.

- Make a pattern of a shell for name tags.

- Collect materials: construction paper, markers, pins, old magazines, large papers, glue, scissors, materials for gift (see below).

- Make copies of the baptismal service for each person.

- Arrange for visit to baptismal font, or

- Arrange to show video of a baptism.

- Set up worship center with white cloth, a pitcher of water, a bowl, small white towel, cross, candle.

The Session

As parents and children enter:

- Make name tags using a shell pattern. Explain that the shell is a symbol of baptism.

- Search through magazines for pictures of water in various forms and being used in different ways. Make a collage by gluing the pictures on a large sheet of paper. Divide them into these categories:

Water gives life	We cannot live without God.
Water cleanses us	God cleans us of wrongs.
Water refreshes us	God refreshes us.

TOGETHER TIME

- Ask families to talk together about times they have been very dirty and how it felt to get cleaned up.

- List on chalkboard or large paper the different uses of water in their pictures. Add any others.

- Explain that we use water as a symbol of baptism. It helps us remember that when we've done something wrong and ask for forgiveness, God forgives, like washing the wrong away.

- Read the story of Jesus' baptism from Matthew 3:13-17.

- Talk about three ways of baptizing (sprinkling, pouring, and immersion), and that with any of these methods we become a part of God's family. Explain to the children that if they were baptized as infants, their parents made certain promises for them, and when they are older they will decide whether to accept the promises for themselves.

- Review the baptismal service, explaining any words not understood.

- Visit baptismal font or view video of baptism.

- While at the baptismal font (or after the video), ask families to share the reminders of baptism that they might have brought.

- Make a gift that can be given at a future baptism. This might be a crib sheet (or pillow case for an older child) with pictures of water drawn on it and something written from each person. Be sure to use permanent markers or fabric crayons and wash the sheet before presenting the gift. (Alternate activity: Make a poster, welcoming the person to the family of God.)

Closing Worship

- Ask if someone can define the word *sacrament*.

- Besides presenting the gift you made, discuss other ways that individuals can welcome someone into God's family when they are baptized (talking with, calling by name, reading or telling Bible stories, and so forth).

- Light candle and remember it symbolizes Christ.

- Hold the pitcher high above the bowl and pour the water so that it makes a splashing sound.

- Sing "I Am the Church! You Are the Church!" As you sing, walk among the families with the bowl, allowing each person to lift a handful of water and let it run back into the bowl.

- Pray: "Our God, we thank you that each of us is a part of your church. We remember that you give us life and forgive our wrongs. Amen."

- Create a cinquain (*sin cane*) poem together, asking persons to give words as you write them:

  Line 1:   Baptism
  Line 2:   Two words about baptism
  Line 3:   Three action words about baptism
  Line 4:   Your "feeling" words telling of baptism (four words)
  Line 5:   One word that means the same as baptism or "Amen"

  Place the words in this order.

  _____

  _____ _____

  _____ _____ _____

  _____ _____ _____ _____

  _____

- Sing "Take My Life and Let It Be."

- Read cinquain poem together.

Resources and References

Resources within text

Broyles, Anne. *Journaling: A Spirit Journey.* Nashville: Upper Room Books, 1988.

Bruce, Barbara. *Seven Ways of Teaching the Bible to Children.* Nashville: Abingdon Press, 1996.

Floyd, Pat. *The Special Days and Seasons of the Christian Year.* Nashville: Abingdon Press, 1998.

Goldsmith, Malcolm. *Knowing Me, Knowing God.* Nashville: Abingdon Press, 1997.

Halverson, Delia. *32 Ways to Become a Great Sunday School Teacher.* Nashville: Abingdon Press, 1997.

Halverson, Delia. *The Gift of Hospitality.* Saint Louis: Chalice Press, 1999.

Halverson, Delia. *How Do Our Children Grow?* Nashville: Chalice Press, 1999.

Halverson, Delia. *How to Train Volunteer Teachers.* Nashville: Abingdon Press, 1991.

Halverson, Delia. *Leading Adult Learners.* Nashville: Abingdon Press, 1995.

Halverson, Delia. *Living Simply.* Nashville: Abingdon Press, 1996.

Harris, Edie and Shirley Ramsey. *Sprouts: Nurturing Children Through Covenant Discipleship.* Nashville: Discipleship Resources, 1996.

MacQueen, Neil. *Computers, Kids and Christian Education.* Minneapolis: Augsburg Fortress Press, 1998.

Mather, Herb. *Don't Shoot the Horse ('til You Know How to Drive the Tractor)—Moving from Annual Fund-Raising to a Life of Giving.* Nashville: Discipleship Resources, 1994.

Morris, Danny, and Charles Olsen. *Discerning God's Will Together.* Nashville: Upper Room Books, 1997.

Norton, MaryJane Pierce. *Children Worship.* Nashville: Discipleship Resources, 1997.

O'Donnell, Michael J. *Being an Acolyte.* Nashville: Discipleship Resources, 1991.

Olsen, Charles. *Transforming Church Boards into Communities of Spiritual Leaders.* Bethesda, Md.: Alban Institute, 1995.

Spence, Nancy, and Jane Connell. *From BC to PC: A Guide for Using Computers with Children in Christian Education.* Nashville: Abingdon Press, 1999.

Sutherland, David C. *Together in Love.* Nashville, Discipleship Resources, 1999.

Watson, David Lowes. *Covenant Discipleship.* Nashville: Discipleship Resources, 1991.

Westerhoff III, John. *Will Our Children Have Faith?* Harrisburg, Penn.: Morehouse, 2000.

• •

Children's Church Times; Abingdon Press (800-672-1789) or via the Internet: www.cokesbury.com.

Complete Bible Lessons for Adults (CD-Rom edited by Delia Halverson); Abingdon Press.

Faith Home; Abingdon Press.

Leader in the Church School Today (quarterly magazine); Abingdon Press.

Pockets; Upper Room.

Goodson, Millie. *Wonderfilled Weekdays: 65 Lesson Plans for Christian Preschool Ministries*; Abingdon Press.

Additional Resources

Brown, Carolyn C. *You Can Preach to the Kids Too!* Nashville: Abingdon Press, 1997.

Cloyd, Betty Shannon. *Children and Prayer*. Nashville: Upper Room Books, 1997.

Cox, William J. *Designing a Single Adult Ministry*. Nashville: Discipleship Resources, 1996.

Crockett, Joseph. *Teaching Scripture from an African-American Perspective*. Nashville: Discipleship Resources, 1990.

Downing, Sue. *Hand in Hand*. Nashville: Discipleship Resources, 1998.

Gentzler, Richard H. Jr. *Designing an Older Adult Ministry*. Nashville: Discipleship Resource, 1999.

Gran, Mary Alice. *The First 3 Years*. Nashville: Discipleship Resources, 1995.

Halverson, Delia. *My Cup Runneth Over (Most of the Time): Devotions for Teachers*. Nashville: Abingdon Press, 1999.

Halverson, Delia. *New Ways to Tell the Old, Old Story*. Nashville: Abingdon Press, 1992 [available through "Books on Demand" from Abingdon 615-749-6311].

Halverson, Delia. *Teaching Prayer in the Classroom*. Nashville: Abingdon Press, 1989 [available through "Books on Demand" from Abingdon 615-749-6311].

Halverson, Sam. *55 Group Building Activities for Youth*. Nashville: Abingdon Press, 1996.

Isbell, Rick and Sue. *Capture the Moment: Building Faith Traditions for Families*. Nashville: Discipleship Resources, 1998.

Ives, Jane P. *Couples Who Care*. Nashville: Discipleship Resources, 1997.

Krau, Carol. *Keeping in Touch: Christian Formation and Teaching*. Nashville: Discipleship Resources, 1999.

Mead, Loren B. *Five Challenges for the Once and Future Church*. Bethesda, Md.: Alban Institute, 1996.

Meagher, Laura. *Teaching Children About Global Awareness*. New York: Crossroad, 1991.

Miller, Craig Kennet & Lia Icaza-Willett. *Culture Shifts*. Nashville: Discipleship Resources, 1998.

Murray, Steven M. *A Guide to the Internet for Churches & Pastors*. Nashville: Discipleship Resources, 1998.

Trimmer, Edward A. *Essentials for Christian Youth (Youth Ministry Handbook)*. Nashville: Abingdon Press, 1994.

Organizations and other helps

Curric-U-Phone (for questions about curriculum) 800-251-8591 or www.cokesbury.com
Rainbows (for children suffering from loss) 1111 Tower Rd., Schaeumburg, IL 60173, 847-310-1880
The Society of St. Andrew   1-800-333-4597
Sunday School Software   1-800-678-1948 www.sundaysoftware.com/index.htm
Workshop Rotation Model   1-800-678-1948

Christian Education Support Groups

If your denomination is not listed here, check with your national headquarters for information.

Association of Christian Church Educators (Disciples of Christ), Becki Nunally, 120 N. 9th St., Zionsville, IN 46077

Association of Presbyterian Church Educators, Sharon Andrews, ACPE Riverview Towers, 1920 S. First St., Minneapolis, MN 55454, 612-338-8032

Association of United Church Educators, Linn Bartling, 10410 Aboite Rd., Roanoke, IN 46783, 219-672-2837

Christian Educators Fellowship (United Methodist), P.O. Box 24930, Nashville TN 37202, 615-749-6870 chedfel@cs.com. You can post questions for discussion on the bulletin board at www.cefumc.org.

Church of the Brethren Association of Christian Educators, RR1 Box 622, East Berlin, PA 17316, 717-292-1861

Evangelical Lutheran Church in America Christian Educators, Division of Congregational Ministries, 800-638-3522 ext. 2557

Index